FREE Study Skills DVD

Dear Customer,

Thank you for your purchase from Mometrix! We consider it an honor and a privilege that you have purchased our product and we want to ensure your satisfaction.

As a way of showing our appreciation and to help us better serve you, we have developed a Study Skills DVD that we would like to give you for FREE. This DVD covers our *best practices* for getting ready for your exam, from how to use our study materials to how to best prepare for the day of the test.

All that we ask is that you email us with feedback that would describe your experience so far with our product. Good, bad, or indifferent, we want to know what you think!

To get your FREE Study Skills DVD, email freedvd@mometrix.com with *FREE STUDY SKILLS DVD* in the subject line and the following information in the body of the email:

- The name of the product you purchased.
- Your product rating on a scale of 1-5, with 5 being the highest rating.
- Your feedback. It can be long, short, or anything in between. We just want to know your impressions and experience so far with our product. (Good feedback might include how our study material met your needs and ways we might be able to make it even better. You could highlight features that you found helpful or features that you think we should add.)
- Your full name and shipping address where you would like us to send your free DVD.

If you have any questions or concerns, please don't hesitate to contact me directly.

Thanks again!

Sincerely,

Jay Willis
Vice President
jay.willis@mometrix.com
1-800-673-8175

Mometrix
TEST PREPARATION
The World's #1 Test Preparation Company

Mometrix
TEST PREPARATION

HiSET Practice Test Preparation Book 2020 & 2021

2 HiSET Exam Practice Tests for All Subjects

Copyright © 2019 by Mometrix Media LLC

All rights reserved. This product, or parts thereof, may not be reproduced, stored in a retrieval system, or transmitted in any form or by any means—electronic, mechanical, photocopy, recording, scanning, or other—except for brief quotations in critical reviews or articles, without the prior written permission of the publisher.

Written and edited by the Mometrix High School Equivalency Test Team

Printed in the United States of America

This paper meets the requirements of ANSI/NISO Z39.48-1992 (Permanence of Paper).

Mometrix offers volume discount pricing to institutions. For more information or a price quote, please contact our sales department at sales@mometrix.com or 888-248-1219.

Mometrix Media LLC is not affiliated with or endorsed by any official testing organization. All organizational and test names are trademarks of their respective owners.

ISBN 13: 978-1-5167-1225-0
ISBN 10: 1-5167-1225-0

Dear Future Exam Success Story

First of all, **THANK YOU** for purchasing Mometrix study materials!

Second, congratulations! You are one of the few determined test-takers who are committed to doing whatever it takes to excel on your exam. **You have come to the right place.** We developed these practice tests with one goal in mind: to deliver you the best possible approximation of the questions you will see on test day.

Standardized testing is one of the biggest obstacles on your road to success, which only increases the importance of doing well in the high-pressure, high-stakes environment of test day. Your results on this test could have a significant impact on your future, and these practice tests will give you the repetitions you need to build your familiarity and confidence with the test content and format to help you achieve your full potential on test day.

Your success is our success

We would love to hear from you! If you would like to share the story of your exam success or if you have any questions or comments in regard to our products, please contact us at **800-673-8175** or **support@mometrix.com**.

Thanks again for your business and we wish you continued success!

Sincerely,
The Mometrix Test Preparation Team

Copyright © 2017 by Mometrix Media LLC. All rights reserved.
Written and edited by the Mometrix Exam Secrets Test Prep Team
Printed in the United States of America

TABLE OF CONTENTS

PRACTICE TEST #1 1
   LANGUAGE ARTS - READING 1
   LANGUAGE ARTS - WRITING 12
   MATHEMATICS 30
   SCIENCE 40
   SOCIAL STUDIES 49

ANSWER KEY AND EXPLANATIONS 58
   LANGUAGE ARTS - READING 58
   LANGUAGE ARTS - WRITING 61
   MATHEMATICS 65
   SCIENCE 69
   SOCIAL STUDIES 72

PRACTICE TEST #2 78
   LANGUAGE ARTS - READING 78
   LANGUAGE ARTS - WRITING 91
   MATHEMATICS 108
   SCIENCE 117
   SOCIAL STUDIES 124

ANSWER KEY AND EXPLANATIONS 132
   LANGUAGE ARTS - READING 132
   LANGUAGE ARTS - WRITING 134
   MATHEMATICS 139
   SCIENCE 145
   SOCIAL STUDIES 152

THANK YOU 159

Practice Test #1

Language Arts - Reading

Questions 1 through 3 are based on the following text:

> Jo's face was a study next day, for the secret rather weighed upon her, and she found it hard not to look mysterious and important. Meg observed it, but did not trouble herself to make inquiries, for she had learned that the best way to manage Jo was by the law of contraries, so she felt sure of being told everything if she did not ask. She was rather surprised, therefore, when the silence remained unbroken, and Jo assumed a patronizing air, which decidedly aggravated Meg, who in turn assumed an air of dignified reserve and devoted herself to her mother. This left Jo to her own devices, for Mrs. March had taken her place as nurse, and bade her rest, exercise, and amuse herself after her long confinement. Amy being gone, Laurie was her only refuge, and much as she enjoyed his society, she rather dreaded him just then, for he was an incorrigible tease, and she feared he would coax the secret from her. (Little Women by Louisa May Alcott)

1. **From what point of view is this passage written?**
    a. First person
    b. Second person
    c. Third person
    d. Fourth person

2. **The phrase "was a study" implies that**
    a. Jo looked jubilant.
    b. Jo looked secretive.
    c. Jo looked disheveled.
    d. Jo looked angry.

3. **What can you infer about Laurie?**
    a. He was stoic.
    b. He was taciturn.
    c. He was unruly.
    d. He was uncanny.

Questions 4 through 7 are based on the following text:

There Will Come Soft Rains

By Sara Teasdale

  There will come soft rains and the smell of the ground,

  And swallows circling with their shimmering sound;

  And frogs in the pools singing at night,

  And wild plum trees in tremulous white;

5 Robins will wear their feathery fire

  Whistling their whims on a low fence-wire;

  And not one will know of the war, not one

  Will care at last when it is done.

  Not one would mind, neither bird nor tree

10 If mankind perished utterly;

  And Spring herself, when she woke at dawn,

  Would scarcely know that we were gone

4. Which line uses personification?
 a. Line 2
 b. Line 4
 c. Line 7
 d. Line 11

5. The "we" used in line 12 refers to
 a. all of mankind.
 b. the victors of the war.
 c. Americans.
 d. the poet and the reader.

6. This poem is an example of a(n)
 a. sonnet.
 b. rhymed verse.
 c. free verse.
 d. lyric.

7. Which of these statements offers the best summary of the poem?
 a. Nature does not care about the affairs of mankind.
 b. It is the government's responsibility to fight a war.
 c. War has a devastating impact on nature.
 d. Wars should not be fought in the spring.

Questions 8-11 address this passage:

One of the key features of the music scene in the past decade has been the increasing popularity of outsiders, especially those with a career. In previous decades, amateur status was seen as a lower calling or, at best, a step on the way to professional status, but many musical insiders now believe that amateurs actually constitute an elite group within the music scene, with greater chances of eventual success. Professionals, once able to fully

devote themselves to the advancement of their musical careers, now find themselves hamstrung by a variety of factors that were not issues even a decade ago, giving the edge to people who do not depend on music for a livelihood. A number of technological, demographic, and economic factors are to blame for this change.

Full-time musicians always had difficulties making ends meet, but these difficulties have been vastly increased by a changing music scene. The increased popularity of electronic music, mega-bands, and other acts that rely heavily on marketing, theatrics, and expensive effects has made it harder than ever for local acts to draw crowds. The decreasing crowds at coffee houses, bars, and other small venues leave the owners without the ability to pay for live music. Amateurs can still play the same coffee houses as ever, and the lack of a hundred-dollar paycheck at the end of the night is hardly noticed. Professionals, however, have to fight more desperately than ever for those few lucrative gigs.

An even bigger factor has been the rise of digital media in general and digital file sharing in particular. People have been trading copies of music for decades, but in the days of analog tapes there was always a loss. The tape one fan burned for another would be of lesser quality than the original, prompting the recipient to go out and buy the album. Now that music fans can make full-quality copies for little or nothing and distribute them all over the world, it can be very hard for bands to make any money on music sales. Again, this does not make much difference to amateurs, but it robs the professionals of what has traditionally been one of their biggest sources of revenue.

All of this results in a situation so dire for professional musicians that their extra experience often doesn't balance out their lack of economic resources. The amateurs are the only ones who can afford to buy new gear and fix broken equipment, keep their cars in working order to get to shows, and pay to promote their shows. The professionals tend to have to fall back on "day jobs," typically at lower rates and with less opportunity for advancement. Even those professional musicians who are able to supplement their incomes with music lessons, wedding shows, and other traditional jobs are often living at such a low level that they cannot afford to buy the professional equipment they need to keep the higher-paying gigs. A fairly skilled amateur, by contrast, may not have the same level of virtuosity but will be able to fake his way through most of what a professional does at a more competitive rate, which will allow him to play professional shows.

8. The author of this essay is mainly

a. arguing for a return to a climate more favorable to professional musicians.
b. examining the causes of the increasing success of amateur musicians over professionals.
c. revealing the psychological toll the current economy takes on professional musicians.
d. disputing the claim that unsuccessful professional musicians simply don't work hard enough.
e. comparing the relative contributions of professional and amateur musicians.

9. Which of the following statements about musicians does the essay most directly support?

a. Bars and coffee houses should be willing to pay a fair wage to professional musicians.
b. The most popular professional bands have not been affected by the changes that plague most professional musicians.
c. It is much easier for amateur musicians to book shows than it was a decade ago.
d. Professional musicians have recently lost some of their most important sources of income.
e. With the shrinking music scenes, it is nearly impossible for a modern musician to support himself on music alone.

10. In his discussion of professional musicians in the last paragraph, the author

a. indicates that amateurs deserve their new, higher status.
b. shows that in the current climate, professionals may not have the ability to purchase and maintain the tools that they need.
c. points out the decrease in the market for wedding gigs and lessons.
d. questions an assumption about the status of professional musicians.
e. predicts a decline in the number of professional musicians.

11. According to the essay, amateur musicians are becoming more successful at both amateur and professional gigs because professionals

a. exclusively performs high-paying gigs and are unwilling to play in clubs.
b. are not able to relate to ordinary people as well as amateurs can.
c. have financial needs that they are not able to meet in the current musical climate.
d. are in an industry that is particularly susceptible to economic changes.
e. don't receive the same respect as people with more lucrative careers.

Questions 12-19 are based on the following passage:

Excerpt of a judicial review summary written by Bernard Schwartz

Judicial review, the power of courts to determine the legality of governmental acts, usually refers to the authority of judges to decide a law's constitutionality. Although state courts exercised judicial review prior to the ratification of the Constitution, the doctrine is most often traced to the landmark U.S. Supreme Court decision Marbury v. Madison (1803), which struck down an act of Congress as unconstitutional. In a now classic opinion, Chief Justice John Marshall found the power of judicial review implied in the Constitution's status as "the supreme Law of the Land" prevailing over ordinary laws.

Both federal and state courts have exercised judicial review. Federal courts review federal and state acts to ensure their conformity to the Constitution and the supremacy of federal over state law; state courts review laws to ensure their conformity to the U.S. Constitution and their own state constitutions. The power of judicial review can be exercised by any court in which a constitutional issue arises.

Judicial review gained added importance in the late nineteenth and early twentieth centuries, as courts passed judgement on laws regulating corporate behavior and working conditions. In these years, the Supreme Court repeatedly struck down laws regulating wages, hours of labor, and safety standards. This is often called the Lochner Era, after Lochner v. New York, a 1905 decision ruling a New York maximum-hours law unconstitutional on the grounds that it violated the Fourteenth Amendment. During this period, the Supreme Court invalidated no fewer than 228 state laws.

Justice Oliver Wendell Holmes Jr., dissenting from many of these decisions, urged judges to defer to legislatures. In the later 1930's, the Supreme Court adopted the Holmes approach-partly in response to the threat of President Franklin Delano Roosevelt's "court packing" plan of 1937. Deferring to legislative judgement, the Supreme Court thereafter upheld virtually all laws regulating business and property rights, including laws similar to those invalidated during the Lochner Era.

Under the chief justiceship of Earl Warren (1953-1969) and beyond, however, the Court moved toward striking down law restricting personal rights and liberties guaranteed by the Bill of Rights, particularly measures limiting freedom of expression, freedom or religion, the right of criminal defendants, equal treatment of the sexes, and the rights of minorities to equal protection of the law. In another extension of judicial review, the Court read new rights into the Constitution, notably the right of privacy (including abortion rights) and invalidated laws restricting those rights. Many other countries including Germany, Italy, France, and Japan, adopted the principle of judicial review after World War II, making constitutional law one the more important recent American exports.

12. Which of the following statements about judicial review does the passage best support?
    a. States should defer to the Federal Government when interpreting the Constitution.
    b. Judicial Review was started due to the Lochner Era.
    c. The Constitution overrides state law in some cases.
    d. The Courts do not have the power to regulate business.
    e. Judicial Review was founded by Earl Warren Chief Justice of the Supreme Court.

13. From the passage, it can be inferred ordinary laws created by lawmakers must be within the framework of the Constitution. Which of the following sentences supports this claim the best?
    a. Although state courts exercised...
    b. Both federal and state courts...
    c. Judicial review gained added importance...
    d. During this period, the Supreme...
    e. Deferring to legislature judgement...

14. Which of the following words best characterizes the content of the passage?
    a. historical
    b. transcription
    c. prospective
    d. figurative
    e. demonstrative

15. The word ratification as used in this passage refers to

a. endorsement
b. disapprove
c. limiting
d. embargo
e. transitional

16. The word dissenting as used in this passage refers to

a. headstrong
b. compatible
c. obliging
d. contradictory
e. exasperation

17. The explanation of judicial review is based on

a. Judicial foresight
b. Constitutional arguments
c. Chief Justice Warren
d. Marbury v Madison
e. Lochner v New York

18. What was Franklin Delano Roosevelt's contribution to the process of Judicial Review according to the summary?

a. The appointment of Earl Warren to the Court
b. Adopted the Holmes approach according to the author
c. Threatened the Court according to the author
d. Upheld laws regulating business
e. Read new rights to the Constitution

19. Which of the following was done during the Lochner Era according to the summary?

a. State laws were struck down repeatedly
b. Judicial Review became accepted
c. Justice Holmes retired
d. The courts were unable to pass judgement on corporate behavior
e. The courts upheld laws regulating wages

Questions 20-23 refer to the following passage:

"His pride," said Miss Lucas, "does not offend me so much as pride often does, because there is an excuse for it. One cannot wonder that so very fine a young man, with family, fortune, everything in his favour, should think highly of himself. If I may so express it, he has a right to be proud."

"That is very true," replied Elizabeth, "and I could easily forgive his pride, if he had not mortified mine."

"Pride," observed Mary, who piqued herself upon the solidity of her reflections, "is a very common failing I believe. By all that I have ever read, I am convinced that it is very common indeed, that human nature is particularly prone to it, and that there are very few of us who do not cherish a feeling of self-complacency on the score of some quality or other, real or imaginary. Vanity and pride are different things, though the words are often used synonymously. A person may be proud without being vain. Pride relates more to our opinion of ourselves, vanity to what we would have others think of us."

20. **Why doesn't the gentleman's pride offend Miss Lucas?**
    a. She admires his vanity.
    b. He offended Elizabeth.
    c. It is human nature to be proud.
    d. He is poor and homeless.
    e. He is handsome and rich.

21. **What are Elizabeth's feelings towards the gentleman?**
    a. She is offended by him.
    b. She enjoys his company.
    c. She is proud of him.
    d. She wants to get to know him better.
    e. She is glad he is rich.

22. **Which sentence best states the theme of this passage?**
    a. Pride and vanity are offensive.
    b. Fame and fortune can make a person proud.
    c. Every person is proud in one way or another.
    d. Pride can bring you fortune.
    e. If you have a fortune, you deserve to be proud.

23. **According to the passage, what is the difference between pride and vanity?**
    a. Pride relates to a person's abilities; vanity relates to a person's looks.
    b. Men are proud; women are vain.
    c. Pride and vanity are synonymous.
    d. Pride is what you think of yourself; vanity is what you want others to think of you.
    e. Pride is part of human nature; vanity is not.

Questions 24-35 refer to the following passage:

Garth

The next morning she realized that she had slept. This surprised her – so long had sleep been denied her! She opened her eyes and saw the sun at the window. And then, beside it in the window, the deformed visage of Garth. Quickly, she shut her eyes again, feigning sleep. But he was not fooled. Presently she heard his voice, soft and kind: "Don't be afraid. I'm your friend. I came to watch you sleep, is all. There now, I am behind the wall. You can open your eyes."

The voice seemed pained and plaintive. The Hungarian opened her eyes, saw the window empty. Steeling herself, she arose, went to it, and looked out. She saw the man below, cowering by the wall, looking grief-stricken and resigned. Making an effort to overcome her revulsion, she spoke to him as kindly as she could.

"Come," she said, but Garth, seeing her lips move, thought she was sending him away. He rose and began to lumber off, his eyes lowered and filled with despair.

"Come!" she cried again, but he continued to move off. Then, she swept from the cell, ran to him and took his arm. Feeling her touch, Garth trembled uncontrollably. Feeling that she drew him toward her, he lifted his supplicating eye and his whole face lit up with joy.

She drew him into the garden, where she sat upon a wall, and for a while they sat and contemplated one another. The more the Hungarian looked at Garth, the more deformities she discovered. The twisted spine, the lone eye, the huge torso over the tiny legs. She couldn't comprehend how a creature so awkwardly constructed could exist. And yet, from the air of sadness and gentleness that pervaded his figure, she began to reconcile herself to it.

"Did you call me back?" asked he.

"Yes," she replied, nodding. He recognized the gesture.

"Ah," he exclaimed. "Do you know that I am deaf?"

"Poor fellow," exclaimed the Hungarian, with an expression of pity.

"You'd think nothing more could be wrong with me," Garth put in, somewhat bitterly. But he was happier than he could remember having been.

24. Why was the girl surprised that she had slept?
   a. It was afternoon.
   b. She seldom slept.
   c. It had been a long time since she had had the chance to sleep.
   d. She hadn't intended to go to sleep.
   e. Garth looked so frightening that she thought he would keep her awake.

25. Why did she shut her eyes again when she saw Garth in the window?
   a. She wanted to sleep some more.
   b. The sun was so bright that it hurt her eyes.
   c. She didn't want to look at Garth.
   d. She wanted Garth to think she was still sleeping.
   e. She was trying to remember how she got there.

26. What two characteristics are contrasted in Garth?
   a. Ugliness and gentleness
   b. Fear and merriment
   c. Distress and madness
   d. Happiness and sadness
   e. Anger and fearfulness

27. During this passage, how do the girl's emotions toward Garth change?
   a. They go from fear to loathing.
   b. They go from anger to fear.
   c. They go from hatred to disdain.
   d. They go from fear to disdain.
   e. They go from revulsion to pity.

28. Why does the girl have to steel herself to approach the window and look out at Garth?
   a. She is groggy from sleep.
   b. She has not eaten for a long time.
   c. She is repelled by his appearance.
   d. She is blinded by the sun behind him.
   e. The window is open and it is cold.

29. How does Garth feel toward the girl when he first moves away from the window?
   a. He is curious about her.
   b. He is sad because she appears to reject him.
   c. He is angry at her for pretending to sleep.
   d. He pretends to be indifferent toward her.
   e. He expects her to scold him.

30. Why does Garth withdraw from the girl when she first speaks to him?
   a. He expects her to hurt him.
   b. He misunderstands her because he cannot hear.
   c. People are always mean to him.
   d. He thinks she wants to sleep some more.
   e. He doesn't want her to feel revulsion because of his appearance.

31. What is a synonym for the word supplicating?
   a. Castigating
   b. Menacing
   c. Repeating
   d. Begging
   e. Steeling

32. Why is it surprising that the girl takes Garth's arm?
   a. She is engaged to someone else.
   b. She has to reach through the window.
   c. He is deaf.
   d. She was very frightened of him initially.
   e. His clothes are dirty.

33. Which of the following adjectives might you use to describe the girl's personality?
   a. Determined
   b. Robust
   c. Manic
   d. Contemplative
   e. Sympathetic

34. Which of the following adjectives would you use to describe Garth's feelings toward himself?
   a. Contemplative
   b. Destitute
   c. Unhappy
   d. Deflated
   e. Jaunty

35. Why is Garth so happy in the last sentence?
  a. Because he can understand the girl.
  b. He has learned to read lips.
  c. Because the girl figured out that he is deaf.
  d. Because the girl seems to accept him.
  e. Because the sun is shining.

Questions 36 through 38 are based on the following text:

Although technological tools like polygraph tests, psychological theories, and interrogation techniques have resulted in slightly greater accuracy for law enforcement agents catching liars, it is still important to understand the nature of lies and check unfounded assumptions that can lead to unquestioning acceptance of false statements. Because intentional deception is one of the biggest obstacles to a successful criminal investigation, developing the ability to separate dubious or outright false statements from true ones has to be one of the main goals of every police officer and law enforcement investigator. In addition, an officer must be able to quickly sort out the possible repercussions of a false statement and the ways it can affect the rest of an investigation, should one slip by police screening. This is the only way to punish the guilty, exonerate the innocent, and do the most possible good in preventing future crimes.

The most difficult lie to catch is the half-truth. Half-truths are distortions constructed by using a seed of truth as a way to sprout a more convincing lie. A half-truth may incorporate intentional exaggeration or understatement, lies of omission, false implications, or outright lies mixed in with actual facts. Half-truths that slip past the detectives investigating a case are classified as either "smoke" lies or "mirror" lies. Smoke refers to half-truths that slow down an investigation by casting doubt on otherwise promising leads or angles of investigation. Mirrors are lies that manage to send the detective off in the wrong direction altogether, usually by linking a fact to a false supposition.

Most other lies are overt and intentional. Usually, they are told as a way for a suspect or witness to protect himself or his friends or, more rarely, to cast suspicion on a rival. In some cases, these sorts of lies can be compounded by overzealous or corrupt police who want to earn a conviction of a supposed perpetrator at any cost. Particularly in high-profile cases with gruesome details, this sort of lie results in more false convictions than any other type of distortion.

36. Which statement most accurately conveys the essay's main idea?
  a. New police techniques have been ineffective at helping investigators catch liars.
  b. The worst lies aren't outright lies, but sneaky half-truths.
  c. People in law enforcement need to be able to recognize lies to be effective and just.
  d. There are only two primary types of lies.
  e. Most overt lies are told to protect a suspect or a witness.

37. The essay's writer would be most likely to say that a police officer's ability to recognize both lies and half-truths is

a. indispensable in a criminal investigation.
b. difficult because of the sophistication of some liars.
c. the most important tool that law enforcement has.
d. important only when investigating a crime.
e. crucial, but beyond the abilities of most officers.

38. According to the essay, "smoke"

a. is the most frequently told type of half-truth.
b. never contains outright lies mixed in with truth.
c. can slow down an investigation.
d. is used to protect the guilty.
e. sends detectives off in the wrong direction altogether.

39. Beowulf is an epic poem that is important because it is often viewed as the first significant work of English literature. Although it was first written in 700A.D., it is thought to be even hundreds of years older than that. It is believed that the story of Beowulf was told for centuries before it ever made its way on to paper. It is still taught today in various schools and universities.

a. Beowulf is a significant poem because
b. it was first written down in 700A.D.
c. it was told for centuries before it was written down.
d. it is still taught today in academic settings.
e. it is the first important work of English literature.

40. According to the laws of supply and demand, consumers will demand less of a good if the price is higher and more if it is lower. Conversely, suppliers will produce more of a good when the price is higher and less when it is lower.

a. If a supplier wanted to sell more of a good, they would
b. reduce the supply.
c. reduce the price.
d. raise the price.
e. increase the supply.

Language Arts - Writing

1. **Where should the following sentence be placed in the paragraph below?**

   Many people have proposed explanations for this drop.

   1] Surveys of criminal activity in the United States have shown that the 1990s marked a significant drop in crimes such as vehicle theft, rape, and murder. 2] Economist Rick Nevin argues that one contributing factor is the ban on lead gasoline in the 70s because lead poisoning in children has been linked with criminal behavior later in life. 3] Other theories include the controversial claim that legalizing abortion has led to fewer unwanted children and, as a result, fewer potential criminals. 4] Some politicians, including Rudy Giuliani, even take personal responsibility, identifying their policies as effective deterrents to crime.

   a. After sentence 1
   b. After sentence 2
   c. After sentence 3
   d. After sentence 4

2. **Where should the following sentence be placed in the paragraph below?**

   Insects that carry the disease can develop resistance to the chemicals, or insecticides, that are used to kill the mosquitoes.

   1] Malaria, a disease spread by insects and parasites, has long proven to be difficult to treat. 2] Part of the explanation has to do with adaptation, or the ability of one generation to pass its strengths on to another. 3] Some insects are simply not affected by these insecticides. 4] Unfortunately, these are the insects that survive and go on to reproduce, creating another generation of insects that are immune to the current insecticides. 5] Many researchers have abandoned hope for insecticides as a cure for malaria, turning their attention instead to other forms of defense, such as protein-blockers that protect humans from the effects of the disease instead of from the carriers.

   a. After sentence 1
   b. After sentence 2
   c. After sentence 3
   d. After sentence 4

3. **Which sentence does not belong in the following paragraph?**

   1] Though Thomas Jefferson's taste for expensive home furnishings and wine contributed to the substantial debts he faced toward the end of his life, many other factors also contributed. 2] For instance, when Jefferson's father-in-law died, all of his debts were transferred to Jefferson. 3] Additionally, though his holdings in land and slaves were considerable, they were never especially profitable. 4] Jefferson is believed to have fathered children with one of his slaves. 5] Finally, less than a decade before his death, Jefferson unwisely agreed to endorse a $20,000 loan for a friend, and when the friend unexpectedly died a year later, Jefferson inherited yet another large debt. 6] Jefferson's personal experience with debt may have been part of his motivation in criticizing policies that would increase the national debt.

   a. Sentence 2
   b. Sentence 3
   c. Sentence 4
   d. Sentence 5

4. **Which sentence does not belong in the following paragraph?**

1] Renowned scientist Richard Feynman once said that the atomic theory is the most profound discoveries scientists have made. 2] Feynman was also an accomplished percussionist who could play nine beats with one hand while playing ten with the other! 3] "All things are made of atoms," explained Feynman, "little particles that...move around in perpetual motion, attracting each other when they are a little distance apart, but repelling upon being squeezed into one another." 4] He then made the claim that this idea is one of the most illuminating ideas in the history of science: "In that one sentence, you will see, there is an enormous amount of information about the world, if just a little imagination and thinking are applied."

a. Sentence 1
b. Sentence 2
c. Sentence 3
d. Sentence 4

Questions 5-9 are based on the following passage:

(1) Kids and people need to spend more time outside on a daily basis. <u>Last Child in the Woods: Saving Our Children from Nature-Deficit Disorder</u> is by Richard Louv and who says that in the last 30 years kids have become increasingly removed from nature to their detriment. (2) A 1991 study found that the radius children are allowed to roam outside their homes has shrunk to 1/9 of what it was 20 years before.

(3) Very bad for their physical fitness and mental health. (4) One in 5 American children is obese—compared with one in 20 in the late 1960s—and nearly 8 million kids suffer from mental illnesses, including depression and attention deficit disorder. (5) He says playing in nature helps reduce stress, increase concentration and promote problem-solving, this can help kids with attention deficit disorder and many other problems. Nature play can increase a child's self confidence and independence.

(6) Parents are scared to let kids play in the woods. (7) Parents are increasingly afraid of child abduction. (8) This is a terrible thing but actually very rare and fear of them should be balanced against the effect of fear on our daily lives.

(9) Kids play too many video games, watch too much television and are in the car for long stretches of time. (10) It is important to have the experience of wet feet and dirty hands and not just read about a frog, for example but to hold it in your hands.

(11) Parents and emphasize organized sports over imaginative play. (12) It's great that kids play so much organized sports now, but activity and physical play used to be what kids did with their free time, not twice a week for soccer practice.

5. **Which version of the following portion of sentence 2 provides the most clarity?** "...is by Richard Louv and who says that in the last 30 years kids have become increasingly removed..."

   a. is by Richard Louv and who says that in the last 30 years kids have become increasingly removed
   b. is by Richard Louv, who says that in the last 30 years kids have become increasingly removed
   c. is by Richard Louv and he says that in the last 30 years kids have become increasingly removed
   d. is by Richard Louv he says that in the last 30 years kids have become increasingly removed
   e. is by Richard Louv and who say in the last 30 years kids have become increasingly removed

6. **Which of the following is the most succinct and clear way to re-write sentences 6 and 7?**

   a. Parents are scared to let kids play in the woods. Parents are increasingly afraid of child abduction.
   b. Parents are scared to let kids play in the woods and are increasingly afraid of child abduction.
   c. Parents are scared to let kids play in the woods because they are increasingly afraid of child abduction.
   d. Parents are scared to let kids play in the woods so they are increasingly afraid of child abduction.
   e. Parents are scared to let kids play in the woods or be abducted.

7. **Which of the following represents the best version of sentence 3?**

   a. Very bad for their physical fitness and mental health.
   b. It is very bad for their physical fitness and mental health.
   c. This is very bad for their physical fitness and mental health.
   d. Which is very bad for their physical fitness and mental health.
   e. This "Nature-Deficit Disorder" is very bad for their physical fitness and mental health.

8. **Sentence 8 is poorly written. What can we infer the initial "This" of the sentence refers to?**

   a. Parents
   b. Kids
   c. Play
   d. Woods
   e. Child abduction

9. **The paragraph that includes sentences 9 and 10 does not contain a clear point. Which of the following best describes what the author is likely trying to communicate in this paragraph?**

   a. Nature is important.
   b. It is a problem that kids are increasingly entertained by technology, rather than by the sensory experience of nature.
   c. It is a problem that kids are increasingly lethargic.
   d. It is a problem that kids are removed from nature.
   e. Kids should get their hands and feet dirty in some way very often.

Questions 10-15 refer to the following passage:

(1)One of the pioneer sculptors of the nineteenth century was Honore Daumier (1810-1879). (2)He is well-known particularly for caricature heads that were created between 1830 and 1832. (3)His later works anticipate the work of Rodin, what with their highly cut-out surfaces offset by studied, flowing poses.

(4)Although Daumier was one of the first modern sculptors, his work did not serve as an influence to later artists. (5)This is because nearly all of the other artists of the time hardly ever got to see any of it. (6)This is also true of the sculpture of Degas, who was known as a painter rather than a sculptor, and whose sculpture also was not widely exhibited at the time. (7)And yet, Degas was clearly the greatest sculptor of the era. (8)His bronze casts of dancers and horses retain the layered feeling of the wax models that were their first versions. (9)His more complex scenes seem like crosses between sculpture and painting. (10)When looked at more closely, they display a feeling of mass that the painted canvas cannot by itself convey. (11)It is the interplay between the separate masses in these scenes that involves the viewer and gives them their sense of intrigue.

10. Which is the best version of the underlined part of sentence 2 (reproduced below)?

<u>He is well-known particularly</u> for caricature heads that were created between 1830 and 1832.

   a. (as it is now)
   b. He is well known, particularly
   c. He is particularly well known
   d. He is well known particularly
   e. He was well-known particularly

11. Which is the best version of the underlined part of sentence 3 (reproduced below)?

His later works anticipate the work <u>of Rodin, what with their highly cut-out surfaces</u> offset by studied, flowing poses.

   a. (as it is now)
   b. of Rodin, what with highly cut-out surfaces
   c. of Rodin; what with highly cut out surfaces
   d. of Rodin, with highly cut-out surfaces
   e. of Rodin, with cut-out surfaces

12. In context, which is the best revision of sentence 5 (reproduced below)?

This is because nearly all of the other artists of the time hardly ever got to see any of it.

   a. (as it is now)
   b. This is because it was almost never exhibited at the time.
   c. His work was hardly ever exhibited.
   d. This is because they hardly ever saw any of it.
   e. This is because it was hardly ever seen by the other artists.

13. In context, which is the best way to revise sentence 6 (reproduced below)?

This is also true of the sculpture of Degas, who was known as a painter rather than a sculptor, and whose sculpture also was not widely exhibited at the time.

    a. Add "In addition," to the beginning of the sentence.
    b. Delete the words ", and whose sculpture was also not widely exhibited at the time."
    c. Change the words "sculpture of Degas" to read "work of Degas".
    d. Change "This is also true" to "This was also true".
    e. Delete the words "rather than a sculptor".

14. Which sentence is best inserted after sentence 7?

    a. A large body of his sculpted works can be found in museums today.
    b. His paintings were famous even before the time of his death.
    c. He wrote several books and articles about art that were read by his contemporaries.
    d. He made sculptures out of bronze, stone, and even wood.
    e. You can see pictures of his work in many books.

15. Which is best added to the beginning of sentence 10?

    a. Increasingly,
    b. And yet,
    c. Beneath this,
    d. However,
    e. It follows that

Questions 16-21 refer to the following passage:

    1) Passports, internationally, are recognized travel documents that verify their bearers' identity and nationality. 2) A valid U.S. passport is required to enter and leave foreign countries. 3) *The only authority to grant issue or verify United States passports* is the United States Department of State (DOS). 4) And it does so through the Passport Services Office. 5) This office of the DOS: Bureau of Consular Affairs (CA) provides information and services to American citizens about obtaining, replacing, renewing or correcting/changing a passport.

    6) You are required to apply in person at any of the over 9,000 passport acceptance facilities located throughout the United States to obtain a passport for the first time. 7) You must provide certain supporting documents and two recent photographs of yourself when you apply or renew. 8) Application forms can be completed online using the Passport Application Wizard, but must be printed prior to submission.

    9) The United States issues both traditional passport books and limited use passport card. 10) You may obtain either one or both of these, depending on your travel needs. 11) Additional information for passports, including answers to frequently asked questions, is available through the DOS: National Passport Information Center (NPIC).

16. Which is the best version of sentence 1?

Passports, internationally, are recognized travel documents that verify their bearers' identity and nationality.

   a. (As it is now)
   b. Passports are recognized documents, internationally, that verify their bearers' identity and nationality.
   c. Passports are internationally recognized travel documents that verify their bearers' identity and nationality.
   d. Internationally, passports are recognized travel documents that verify its bearers' identity and nationality.
   e. Passports are internationally recognized travel documents that verify their bearers identity and nationality.

17. Which is the best version of the italicized part of sentence 3?

The only authority to grant issue or verify United States passports is the United States Department of State (DOS).

   a. (As it is now)
   b. The only authority to grant, issue or verify United States passports
   c. The only authority to grant, issue, or verify United States Passports
   d. The only authority to grant, issue, or verify United States passports
   e. The only authority to grant, issue, or verify United States passport

18. What is the best way to write the last part of sentence 3 and all of sentence 4?

The only authority to grant issue or verify United States passports is the United States Department of State (DOS). And it does so through the Passport Services Office.

   a. (As it is now)
   b. is the Department of State (DOS): and it does so through the Passport Services Office.
   c. is the Department of State (DOS); and it does so through the Passport Services Office.
   d. is the Department of State (DOS), And it does so through the Passport Services Office.
   e. is the Department of State (DOS), and it does so through the Passport Services Office.

19. In context, which of the following is the correct way to phrase sentence 6?

You are required to apply in person at any of the over 9,000 passport acceptance facilities located throughout the United States to obtain a passport for the first time.

   a. (As it is now)
   b. To obtain a passport for the first time you are required to apply in person at any of the over 9,000 passport acceptance facilities located throughout the United States.
   c. To obtain a passport for the first time, you are required to apply in person at any of the over 9,000 passport acceptance facilities located throughout the United States.
   d. You are required to apply in person, at any of the over 9,000 passport acceptance facilities located throughout the United States, to obtain a passport for the first time.
   e. At any of the over 9,000 passport acceptance facilities located throughout the United States, you are required to apply in person to obtain a passport for the first time.

20. What is the best version of sentence 9?

The United States issues both traditional passport books and limited use passport card.

a. (As it is now)
b. The United States issues both traditional passport books and limited use passport cards.
c. The United States issue both traditional passport books and limited use passports card.
d. The United States issues both traditional passport books and limited use's passport card.
e. The United States issues both traditional, passport books and limited use passport card.

21. Which sentence is best inserted after sentence 11?

Additional information for passports, including answers to frequently asked questions, is available through the DOS: National Passport Information Center (NPIC).

a. You will probably have to stand in line for a long time.
b. Application forms can be printed online using the Passport Application Wizard.
c. For more information, you can go online at www.travel.state.gov.
d. It takes longer than usual for passports to be issued.
e. Remember to get your picture taken for your passport.

Questions 22-27 refer to the following passage:

1) The Atlantic hurricane season officially runs from June 1 to November 30. 2) With peak activity occurring August through October. 3) When applied to hurricanes, "Atlantic" generally refers to the entire Atlantic Basin, *which included the North Atlantic Ocean*, *Caribbean Sea* and *the Gulf of Mexico*. 4) To view current tropical weather outlooks and public advisories, please visit the National Hurricane Center's (NHC) website.

5) For storm information specific to your area in the United States, including possible inland watches and warnings, please monitor your local weather office. 6) For storm information specific to your area outside of the United States, please monitor products issued by your national meteorological service.

7) In the August 2010 update to the Atlantic hurricane season outlook, the National Oceanic and Atmospheric Administration (NOAA) predicted 14 to 20 named storms, of which eight to 12 could become hurricanes, including four to six major hurricanes of Category 3 strength or higher. 8) The May outlook called for 14 to 23 named storms, including eight to 14 hurricanes and three to seven major hurricanes. 9) Tropical systems acquire a name upon reaching tropical storm strength with sustained winds of at least 39 mph. 10) *Tropical storms become hurricanes with winds reach 74 mph*, and become major hurricanes when winds reach 111 mph. 11) With six becoming hurricanes, including two major hurricanes, an average season has 11 named storms.

22. Which is the best version of sentence 1 and 2?

The Atlantic hurricane season officially runs from June 1 to November 30. With peak activity occurring August through October.

a. (As it is now)
b. The Atlantic hurricane season, officially runs from June 1 to November 30 with peak activity occurring August through October.
c. The Atlantic hurricane season officially runs from June 1 to November 30; with peak activity occurring August through October.
d. The Atlantic hurricane season officially runs from June 1 to November 30, with peak activity occurring August through October.
e. The Atlantic hurricane season officially runs, from June 1 to November 30, with peak activity occurring August through October.

23. Which is the correct version of the italicized part of sentence 3?

When applied to hurricanes, "Atlantic" generally refers to the entire Atlantic Basin, *which included the North Atlantic Ocean, Caribbean Sea and the Gulf of Mexico.*

a. (As it is now)
b. which includes the North Atlantic Ocean, Caribbean Sea and the Gulf of Mexico.
c. which will include the North Atlantic Ocean, Caribbean Sea and the Gulf of Mexico.
d. which has included the North Atlantic Ocean, Caribbean Sea and the Gulf of Mexico.
e. which including the North Atlantic Ocean, Caribbean Sea and the Gulf of Mexico

24. Which is the best version of sentence 5?

For storm information specific to your area in the United States, including possible inland watches and warnings, please monitor your local weather office.

a. (As it is now)
b. Including possible inland watches, for storm information specific to your area in the United States, and warnings please monitor your local weather office.
c. For storm information specific to your area in the United States; including possible inland watches and warnings please monitor your local weather office.
d. For storm information specific to your area in the United States including possible inland watches, and warnings please monitor your local weather office.
e. For storm information specific to your area in the United States including possible inland watches and warnings: please monitor your local weather office.

25. Which choices would be a good sentence after sentence 9?

Tropical systems acquire a name upon reaching tropical storm strength with sustained winds of at least 39 mph.

a. Typhoons occur in the Pacific Ocean.
b. To view current tropical weather outlooks and public advisories, please visit the National Hurricane Center's (NHC) website.
c. The naming of tropical storms and hurricanes began in 1953 when the National Weather Service gave the storms female names.
d. NOAA updates its storm predictions regularly.
e. It is best to seek shelter during a hurricane.

26. Which of the following is the correct version of the italicized part of sentence 10?

Tropical storms become hurricanes with winds reach 74 mph and become major hurricanes when winds reach 111 mph.

  a. (As it is now)
  b. Tropical storms become hurricanes since winds reach 74 mph
  c. Tropical storms become hurricanes toward winds reach 74 mph
  d. Tropical storms become hurricanes when winds reach 74 mph
  e. Tropical storms become hurricanes around winds reach 74 mph

27. In context, which of the following is the best version of sentence 11?

With six becoming hurricanes, including two major hurricanes, an average season has 11 named storms.

  a. (As it is now)
  b. An average season has 11 named storms, with six becoming hurricanes, including two major hurricanes.
  c. With six becoming hurricanes including two major hurricanes, an average season has 11 named storms.
  d. An average season has 11 named storms, with six becoming hurricanes includes two major hurricanes.
  e. An average season has 11 named storms. With six becoming hurricanes, including two major hurricanes.

Questions 28-33 refer to the following passage

> 1) The observance of Halloween (All Hallow's Eve) on October 31 has long been associated with images of witches, ghosts, devils and hobgoblins. 2) The holiday dates back to the Celtic festival of Samhain thousands of years ago. 3) The Celts believed that at the time of Samhain the *ghosts of the dead were able to mingle with the living.* 4) *Because that was when the souls of those who had died during the year traveled into the otherworld.*
>
> 5) Over the years Halloween customs and rituals have changed. 6) Today, many Americans celebrate the traditions of Halloween by dressing in costumes and telling tales of witches and ghosts. 7) Pumpkins are carved and children go from house to house, *knocking on doors and calling out "trick or treat" hoping to have their bags filled with candy.* 8) Many communities also celebrate Halloween by holding local parties and parades.

28. Which is the best version of sentence 1?

The observance of Halloween (All Hallow's Eve) on October 31 has long been associated with images of witches, ghosts, devils and hobgoblins.

   a. (As it is now)
   b. The observance of Halloween (All Hallow's Eve), on October 31 has long been associated with images of witches, ghosts, devils and hobgoblins.
   c. The observance of Halloween (All Hallow's Eve) on October 31 has long been associated with images of witches, ghosts', devils and hobgoblins.
   d. The observance of Halloween (All Hallow's Eve) on October 31 has long been associated with images of witches, ghosts, devils and hobgoblin.
   e. The observance of Halloween, (All Hallow's Eve) on October 31 has long been associated with images of witches, ghosts, devils and hobgoblins.

29. Which is the best version of sentence 2?

The holiday dates back to the Celtic festival of Samhain thousands of years ago.

   a. (As it is now)
   b. The holiday dates back, to the Celtic festival of Samhain thousands of years ago.
   c. The holiday dates back to the Celtic Festival of Samhain thousands of years ago.
   d. The holiday date back to the Celtic Festival of Samhain thousands of years ago.
   e. The holiday dates back to the Celtic festival of Samhain thousands, of years ago.

30. What is the best way to write the italicized part of sentences 3 and 4?

The Celts believed that at the time of Samhain the *ghosts of the dead were able to mingle with the living. Because that was when the souls of those who had died during the year traveled into the otherworld.*

   a. (As it is now)
   b. ghosts of the dead were able to mingle with the living, because that was when the souls, of those who had died during the year, traveled into the otherworld.
   c. ghosts of the dead were able to mingle with the living, because that was when the souls of those who had died during the year traveled into the otherworld.
   d. ghosts of the dead were able to mingle with the living. Because, that was when the souls of those who had died during the year traveled into the otherworld.
   e. ghosts of the dead were able to mingle with the living, because that was when the souls of those who had died during the year travel into the otherworld.

31. In context, which is the best version of sentence 5?

Over the years Halloween customs and rituals have changed.

   a. (As it is now)
   b. Over the years, Halloween customs, and rituals have changed.
   c. Halloween customs and rituals have changed, over the years.
   d. Over the years, halloween customs and rituals have changed.
   e. Over the years, Halloween customs and rituals have changed.

32. What is the best way to write the italicized part of sentence 7?

Pumpkins are carved and children go from house to house, *knocking on doors and calling out "trick or treat" hoping to have their bags filled with candy.*

a. (As it is now)
b. knocking on doors and calling out trick or treat, hoping to have their bags filled with candy.
c. knocking on doors and calling out "trick or treat," hoping to have their bags filled with candy.
d. knocking on doors and calling out "trick or treat," hoping to have their bags fill with candy.
e. knocking on doors, and calling out "trick or treat" hoping to have their bags filled with candy.

33. Which would be the best sentence to use before sentence 8?

Many communities also celebrate Halloween by holding local parties and parade.

a. There are lots of adults that enjoy celebrating Halloween just as much as children.
b. There are lots of adults which enjoy celebrating Halloween just as much as children.
c. Just as much as children there are lots of adults who enjoy celebrating Halloween.
d. There are lots of adults who enjoy celebrating Halloween just as much as children.
e. There are lots of adults, who enjoy celebrating Halloween just as much as children.

Questions 34-40 refer to the following passage:

1) A new car is second only to a home as the most expensive purchase that many consumers make. 2) According to the National Automobile Dealers Association, the average price of a new car sold in the United States as of February 2010 was $28,400. 3) That's why it's important to know how to make a smart deal.

4) Think about what car model and options you want and how much you're willing to spend. 5) Do some research. 6) If you do, *you'll be less likely to feel pressured making a hasty or expensive decision at the showroom* and more likely to get a better deal.

7) To get the best possible price by comparing models and prices in ads and at dealer showrooms shop around. 8) You also may want to contact car-buying service and broker-buying service to make comparisons.

9) Plan to negotiate on price. 10) Dealers may be willing to bargain on their profit margin which is often between 10 and 20 percent. 11) Usually, this is the difference between the manufacturer's suggested retail price (MSRP) and the invoice price.

12) *Because the price is a factor in the dealer's calculations regardless of whether you pay cash or finance your car — and also affects your monthly payments —* negotiating the price can save you money.

34. Which is best added to the beginning of sentence 1?

A new car is second only to a home as the most expensive purchase many consumers make.

a. However
b. Although
c. Increasingly
d. For example
e. Rarely

35. In context, which is the best version of sentence 2?

According to the National Automobile Dealers Association, the average price of a new car sold in the United States as of February 2010 was $28,400.

   a. (As it is now)
   b. The average price, according to the National Automobile Dealers Association, of a new car sold in the United States as of February 2010 was $28,400.
   c. According to the National Automobile Dealers Association a new car sold in the United States as of February 2010, was $28,400, the average price.
   d. Sold in the United States as of February 2010 was $28,400, accordingly to the National Automobile Dealers Association, the average price of a new car.
   e. The average price of a new car, according to the National Automobile Dealers Association, in the United States sold as of February 2010 was $28,400.

36. What is the best way to write the italicized part of sentence 6?

If you do, *you'll be less likely to feel pressured making a hasty or expensive decision at the showroom* and more likely to get a better deal.

   a. (As it is now)
   b. you'll be less likely to feel pressures making a hasty or expensive decision at the showroom
   c. you'll be less likely to feel pressured into making a hasty or expensive decision at the showroom
   d. you be less likely to feel pressured into making a hasty or expensive decision at the showroom
   e. you'll be less likely to feel pressured into making an hasty or expensive decision at the showroom

37. In context, which is the best version of sentence 7?

To get the best possible price by comparing models and prices in ads and at dealer showrooms shop around.

   a. (As it is now)
   b. By comparing models and prices in ads and at dealer showrooms, shop around, to get the best possible price.
   c. To get the best possible price in ads and at dealer showrooms shop around by comparing models and prices.
   d. In ads and at dealer showrooms shop around to get the best possible price by comparing models and prices.
   e. Shop around to get the best possible price by comparing models and prices in ads and at dealer showrooms.

38. Which is the best version of sentence 8?

You also may want to contact car-buying service and broker-buying service to make comparisons.

a. (As it is now)
b. You also may want to contact car-buying services and broker-buying services to make comparisons.
c. You also may want to contract car-buying services and broker-buying services to make comparisons.
d. You also may want to contact car-buying services, and broker-buying services, to make comparisons.
e. You'll also may want to contact car-buying services and broker-buying services to make comparisons.

39. In context, which is the best version of sentence 10?

Dealers may be willing to bargain on their profit margin which is often between 10 and 20 percent.

a. (As it is now)
b. Often between 10 and 20 percent, dealers may be willing to bargain on their profit margin.
c. Dealers may be willing to bargain on their profit margin, which is often between 10 and 20 percent.
d. To bargain on their profit margin dealers may be willing, often between 10 and 20 percent.
e. Often between 10 and 20 percent dealers may be willing to bargain on their profit margin.

40. What is the best way to write the italicized part of sentence 12?

Because the price is a factor in the dealer's calculations regardless of whether you pay cash or finance your car — and also affects your monthly payments — negotiating the price can save you money.

a. (As it is now)
b. Because the price is a factor in the dealer's calculations regardless of whether you pay cash or finance your car, and also affects your monthly payments,
c. Because the price is a factor in the dealer's calculations, regardless of whether you pay cash or finance your car (it also affects your monthly payments),
d. Because the price is a factor in the dealers calculations, regardless of whether you pay cash or finance your car, and also affects your monthly payments —
e. Because the price is a factor in the dealer's calculations regardless of whether you pay cash or finance your car; and also affects your monthly payments —

Questions 41- 46 refer to the following passage

1) New rules limit the fees that banks and other financial institutions can charge on some services, *so it's possibly that the costs of other services could go up.* 2) In the spring 2010 issue of FDIC Consumer News, we discussed how to avoid potential interest rate and fee increases for credit cards. 3)*And here, from expectations that banks will be adding new fees or requirements on bank accounts* — such as by discontinuing or limiting free checking services — we focus on ways that careful consumers can avoid unnecessary costs on their deposit accounts.

4) Comparison shop so you don't pay more for accounts than you have to. 5) Look at what is being offered by your bank and a few competitors. 6) *If your bank is among those that eliminates its free checking services,* you may still be able to find another

bank offering them, especially if you sign up for direct deposit or electronic statements, or if you conduct a certain number of transactions each month.

7) *In today's low-interest rate environment, it must be better to choose a free account that pays no interest* or only a small amount of interest instead of selecting an account that pays a modest interest rate but imposes a monthly fee. 8) Similarly, it may be better to maintain a balance and avoid a monthly fee rather than putting that money in an account and paying a modest interest rate. 9) In both cases, any interest you would earn will probably be a lot less than the monthly fee, which can be $10 or higher.

41. What is the best way to write the italicized part of sentence 1?

New rules limit the fees that banks and other financial institutions can charge on some services, *so it's possibly that the costs of other services could go up.*

  a. (As it is now)
  b. so it's possible that the costs of other services could go up.
  c. so it's possible that the costs of other services can go up.
  d. then it's possible that the costs of other services could go up.
  e. so it's possibility that the costs of other services could go up.

42. Which is the best way to write the italicized part of sentence 3?

And here, from expectations that banks will be adding new fees or requirements on bank accounts — such as by discontinuing or limiting free checking services — we focus on ways that careful consumers can avoid unnecessary costs on their deposit accounts.

  a. (As it is now)
  b. And here, from expectations that banks will be adding new fees or requirements within bank accounts
  c. And here, with expectations that banks will be adding new fees or requirements on bank accounts
  d. And here, besides expectations that banks will be adding new fees or requirements on bank accounts
  e. And then, with expectations that banks will be adding new fees or requirements on bank accounts

43. Which is the best version of sentence 4?

Comparison shop so you don't pay more for accounts than you have to.

  a. (As it is now)
  b. Comparison shop so you don't paying more for accounts than you have to.
  c. Comparison shop so you don't pays more for accounts than you have to.
  d. Comparison shop so you didn't pay more for accounts than you have to.
  e. Comparison shop so you don't pay no more for accounts than you have to.

44. What is the best way to write the italicized part of sentence 6?

If your bank is among those that eliminates its free checking services, you may still be able to find another bank offering them, especially if you sign up for direct deposit or electronic statements, or if you conduct a certain number of transactions each month.

   a. (As it is now)
   b. If your bank is among those that eliminates its free checking services;
   c. If your bank is within those that eliminates its free checking services,
   d. If your bank is among those that eliminate its free checking services,
   e. If your bank is among those that eliminates it's free checking services,

45. What is the best way to write the italicized part of sentence 7?

In today's low-interest rate environment, it must be better to choose a free account that pays no interest or only a small amount of interest instead of selecting an account that pays a modest interest rate but imposes a monthly fee.

   a. (As it is now)
   b. In today's low-interest rate environment, it might be better to choose a free account that pays no interest
   c. It might be better to choose a free account that pays no interest, in today's low-interest rate environment,
   d. In today's low-interest rate environment, it might be better to have chosen a free account that pays no interest
   e. In today's low-interest rate environment, it might be gooder to choose a free account that pays no interest

46. In context, which is the best version of sentence 9?

In both cases, any interest you would earn will probably be a lot less than the monthly fee, which can be $10 or higher.

   a. (As it is now)
   b. Any interest you would earn is probably a lot less than the monthly fee, which can be $10 or higher, in both cases.
   c. In both cases, any interest you would earn will probably be a lot less then the monthly fee, which can be $10 or higher.
   d. In both cases, any interest you would earn will probably be a lot less than the monthly fee, which can be 10 Dollars or higher.
   e. In any cases, any interest you would earn will probably be a lot less than the monthly fee, which could be $10 or higher.

Questions 47-50 refer to the following passage

> 1) The United States Department of Agriculture Forest Service has reached a milestone. 2) It now protects more than two million acres of private forests threatened by development. 3) *The Forest Service's Northeastern Area helped the agency reach the milestone* when the state of Ohio purchased a 15,494-acre property as the new Vinton Furnace State Experimental Forest approximately 90 miles south of Columbus. 4) The milestone was achieved through public-private partnership *using federal and leveraged funds of approximately $1.1 billion through the Forest legacy program.* 5) The Legacy program has leveraged the federal investment of

more than 50 percent of project costs. 6) To date, through non-federal matching funds, to these efforts, more than $630 million has been contributed.

7) The Forest Legacy program works with private landowners, states and conservation groups to promote sustainable, working forests. 8) Roughly 57 percent of the nation's forests are privately owned, yet the country has lost 15 million acres of private working forests in the last 10 years, with an additional 22 million acres projected to be at risk in the next decade. 9) The Forest Legacy has protected millions of acres of privately owned forests that could have been turned into strip malls and housing developments, say Forest Service experts. 10) They say there have been many success stories, which they are proud of.

47. Which is the best version of sentence 2?
It now protects more than two million acres of private forests threatened by development.

   a. (As it is now)
   b. It now protect more than two million acres of private forests threatened by development.
   c. It now has protected more than two million acres of private forests threatened by development.
   d. It now protecting more than two million acres of private forests threatened by development.
   e. It now has been protecting more than two million acres of private forests threatened by development.

48. Which is the best version of the italicized part of sentence 3?
The Forest Service's Northeastern Area helped the agency reach the milestone when the state of Ohio purchased a 15,494-acre property as the new Vinton Furnace State Experimental Forest approximately 90 miles south of Columbus.

   a. (As it is now)
   b. The Forest Services Northeastern Area helped the agency reach the milestone
   c. The Forest Services Northeastern Area helped the agency reaching the milestone
   d. The Forests' Services Northeastern Area helped the agency reach the milestone
   e. The Forest Services Northeastern Area helped the agency reach a milestones

49. Which is the best version of the italicized part of sentence 4?
The milestone was achieved through public-private partnership *using federal and leveraged funds of approximately $1.1 billion through the Forest legacy program.*

   a. (As it is now)
   b. using federal and leveraged funds of approximately $1.1 billion through the forest legacy program.
   c. using federal and leveraged funds of approximately $1.1 billion through The Forest legacy program.
   d. using federal and leveraged funds of approximately $1.1 billion through the Forest Legacy program.
   e. using federal and leveraged funds of approximately $1.1 billion through the forest Legacy program.

50. In context, which is the best version of sentence 6?

To date, through non-federal matching funds, to these efforts, more than $630 million has been contributed.

    a. (As it is now)
    b. To date, more than $630 million has been contributed to these efforts through non-federal matching funds.
    c. Through non-federal matching funds, to these efforts, more than $630 million, to date, has been contributed.
    d. To these efforts, through non-federal matching funds, more than $630 million has been contributed, to date.
    e. Through non-federal matching funds, more than $630 million to these efforts, to date, has been contributed.

Essay

Merit pay for teachers is the practice of giving increased pay based upon the improvement in student performance. It is a controversial idea among educators and policy makers. Those who support this idea say that, with it, school districts are able to select and retain the best teachers and to improve student performance. Others argue that merit pay systems lead to teacher competition for the best students and to test-driven teaching practices that are detrimental to the overall quality of education.

In your essay, select either of these points of view, or suggest an alternative approach, and make a case for it. Use specific reasons and appropriate examples to support your position and to show how it is superior to the others.

Mathematics

1. If $10x + 2 = 7$, what is the value of $2x$?

    a. 0.5
    b. -0.5
    c. 1
    d. 5
    e. 10

2. A long distance runner does a first lap around a track in exactly 50 seconds. As she tires, each subsequent lap takes 20% longer than the previous one. How long does she take to run 3 laps?

    a. 180 seconds
    b. 182 seconds
    c. 160 seconds
    d. 72 seconds
    e. 150 seconds

3. A number N is multiplied by 3. The result is the same as when N is divided by 3. What is the value of N?

    a. 1
    b. 0
    c. -1
    d. 3
    e. -3

4.

y	-4	31	4	68	12
x	-2	3	0	4	2

Which of the following equations satisfies the five sets of numbers shown in the above table?

   a. $y = 2x^2 + 7$
   b. $y = x^3 + 4$
   c. $y = 2x$
   d. $y = 3x + 1$
   e. $y = 6x$

5. John buys 100 shares of stock at $100 per share. The price goes up by 10% and he sells 50 shares. Then, prices drop by 10% and he sells his remaining 50 shares. How much did he get for the last 50?

    a. $5000
    b. $5500
    c. $4900
    d. $5050
    e. $4950

6. The sides of a triangle are equal to integral numbers of units. Two sides are 4 and 6 units long, respectively; what is the minimum value for the triangle's perimeter?

   a. 10 units
   b. 11 units
   c. 12 units
   d. 13 units
   e. 9 units

7.

Lemons	35%
Sugar	20%
Cups	25%
Stand improvements	5%
Profits	15%

Herbert plans to use the earnings from his lemonade stand according to the table above, for the first month of operations. If he buys $70 worth of lemons, how much profit does he take home?

   a. $15
   b. $20
   c. $30
   d. $35.50
   e. $40

8. A teacher has 3 hours to grade all the papers submitted by the 35 students in her class. She gets through the first 5 papers in 30 minutes. How much faster does she have to work to grade the remaining papers in the allotted time?

   a. 10%
   b. 15%
   c. 20%
   d. 25%
   e. 30%

9. A sailor judges the distance to a lighthouse by holding a ruler at arm's length and measuring the apparent height of the lighthouse. He knows that the lighthouse is actually 60 feet tall. If it appears to be 3 inches tall when the ruler is held 2 feet from his eye, how far away is it?

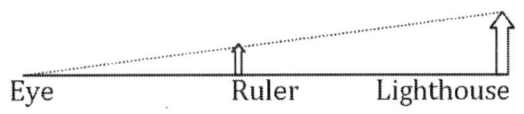

   a. 60 feet
   b. 120 feet
   c. 240 feet
   d. 480 feet
   e. 960 feet

10. If $x^2 - 4 = 45$, then x could be equal to
   a. 9
   b. 5
   c. 3
   d. -4
   e. -7

11. What is the value of the product of the first two prime numbers that are larger than 10 divided by the largest prime number smaller than 30? Use the grids on the answer sheet page where you have answered.

12. Determine the volume of a rectangular box with a length of 5 inches, a height of 7 inches, and a width of 9 inches.
   a. 445.095 in.3
   b. 315 in.3
   c. 45 in.3
   d. 35 in.3
   e. 21 in.3

13. What is the greatest integer value of y for which $5y - 20 < 0$?
   a. 5
   b. 4
   c. 3
   d. 2
   e. 1

14. A commuter survey counts the people riding in cars on a highway in the morning. Each car contains only one man, only one woman, or both one man and one woman. Out of 25 cars, 13 contain a woman and 20 contain a man. How many contain both a man and a woman?

15. Which equation is represented by the graph shown below?

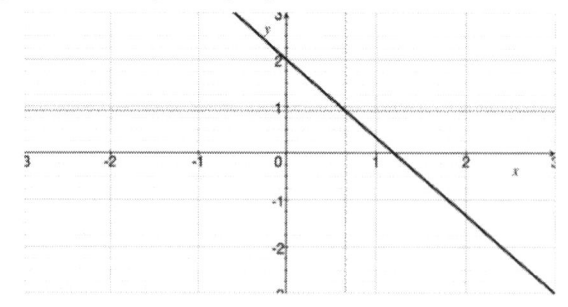

a. $y = \frac{5}{3}x + 2$
b. $y = -\frac{5}{3}x - 2$
c. $y = -\frac{5}{3}X = 2$
d. $y = \frac{5}{3}x - 2$
e. $y = 5x + 2$

16. If x is a negative integer and $5 < |x - 3| < 7$, what is the value of $|x|$?

17. The right circular cylinder shown in the figure below has a height of 10 units and a radius of 1 unit. Points O and P are the centers of the top and bottom surfaces, respectively. A slice is cut from the cylinder as shown, so that the angle at the top, O, is 60 degrees, and the angle at the bottom, P, is 60 degrees. What is the volume of the slice?

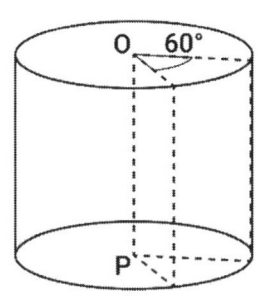

    a. 31.4 units
    b. 5.23 units
    c. 10.47 units
    d. 7.85 units
    e. 15.7 units

18. For the number set {7, 12, 5, 16, 23, 44, 18, 9, Z}, which of the following values could be equal to Z if Z is the median of the set?

    a. 14
    b. 11
    c. 12
    d. 17
    e. 21

19. If Q is divisible by 2 and 7, which of the following is also divisible by 2 and 7?

    a. Q + 2
    b. Q + 7
    c. Q + 28
    d. Q + 9
    e. Q + 11

20. There are 400 fish in a tank. 150 are blue, 150 are red, and the remainder are brown. Tranh dips a net into the tank and pulls out one fish. The probability of pulling out any single fish is the same. What is the probability, in percent, that the fish he pulls out is brown?

21. If a = 3 and b = -2, what is the value of a2 + 3ab – b2?

    a. 5
    b. -13
    c. -4
    d. -20
    e. 13

22. Jack and Kevin play in a basketball game. If the ratio of points scored by Jack to points scored by Kevin is 4 to 3, which of the following could NOT be the total number of points scored by the two boys?

   a. 7
   b. 14
   c. 16
   d. 28
   e. 35

23. Factor the following expression: x2 + x – 12

   a. (x – 4) (x + 4)
   b. (x – 2) (x + 6)
   c. (x + 6) (x – 2)
   d. (x – 4) (x + 3)
   e. (x + 4) (x – 3)

24. Five less than three times a number is equal to 58. What is the number?

25. The average of six numbers is 4. If the average of two of those numbers is 2, what is the average of the other four numbers?

   a. 5
   b. 6
   c. 7
   d. 8
   e. 9

26. In a rectangular x,y coordinate system, what is the intersection of two lines formed by the equations $y = 2x + 3$ and $y = x - 5$?

   a. (5, 3)
   b. (8, 13)
   c. (-4, 13)
   d. (-8, -13)
   e. (2, -7)

27. A function f(x) is defined by $f(x) = 2x^2 + 7$. What is the value of $2f(x) - 3$?

   a. $4x^2 + 11$
   b. $4x^4 + 11$
   c. $x^2 + 11$
   d. $4x^2 + 14$
   e. $2x^2 + 14$

28. The two shortest sides of a right triangle are 6 and 8 units long, respectively. What is the length of the perimeter?

   a. 10 units
   b. 18 units
   c. 24 units
   d. 14 units
   e. 36 units

29. If p and n are positive consecutive integers such that p > n, and $p + n = 15$, what is the value of n?

   a. 5
   b. 6
   c. 7
   d. 8
   e. 9

30. What is the area of a square inscribed in a circle of radius r?

   a. r^2
   b. $2r^2$
   c. $2r^3$
   d. $2\pi r$
   e. $4r^2$

31. Forty students in a class take a test that is graded on a scale of 1 to 10. The histogram in the figure shows the grade distribution, with the x-axis representing the grades and the y-axis representing the number of students obtaining each grade. If the mean, median, and modal values are represented by n, p, and q, respectively, which of the following is true?

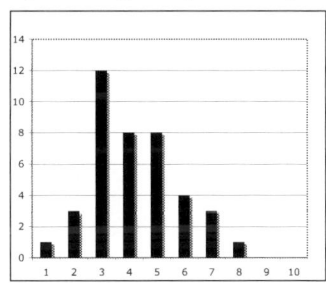

   a. n > p > q
   b. n > q > p
   c. q > p > n
   d. p > q > n
   e. q > n > p

32. If x and y are positive integers, which of the following expressions is equivalent to $(xy)^{7y} - (xy)^y$?

   a. $xy)^{6y}$
   b. $(xy)^{7y-1}$
   c. $(xy)^y[(xy)^7 - 1]$
   d. $(xy)^y[(xy)^{6y} - 1]$
   e. $(xy)^{7y}$

33. The average of 3 numbers x, y, and z is 23. The average of three numbers a, b, and c is also 23. What is the average of all six numbers a, b, c, x, y, and z?

   a. 11.5
   b. 23
   c. 34.5
   d. 46
   e. 5.25

34. In the system of equations below, what is the value of 2x + y?

$$2x + y + 7a = 50$$

$$2x + y + 5a = 40$$

35. If $(6a)x^2 = 30$, then ax^2

   a. 6
   b. 5
   c. 30
   d. $\frac{\sqrt{30}}{6}$
   e. 3

36. In a game played with toothpicks, players A and B take turns removing toothpicks from a row on a table. At each turn, each player must remove 1, 2, or 3 toothpicks from the row. The object is to force the other player to remove the last toothpick. If there are 6 toothpicks in the row, which of the following moves ensures a win?

   a. Remove 1
   b. Remove 2
   c. Remove 3
   d. Remove 1 or 2
   e. There is no way to ensure a win

37. Determine the perimeter of a rectangle with a length of 5 inches and a height of 7 inches.

38. A water sprinkler covers a circular area with a radius of 6 feet. If the water pressure is increased so that the radius increases to 8 feet, by approximately how much is the area covered by the water increased?

   a. 2 square feet
   b. 4 square feet
   c. 36 square feet
   d. 64 square feet
   e. 88 square feet

39. The graph below, not drawn to scale, shows a straight line passing through the origin. Point P1 has the (x,y) coordinates (-5,-3). What is the x-coordinate of point P2 if its y-coordinate is 3?

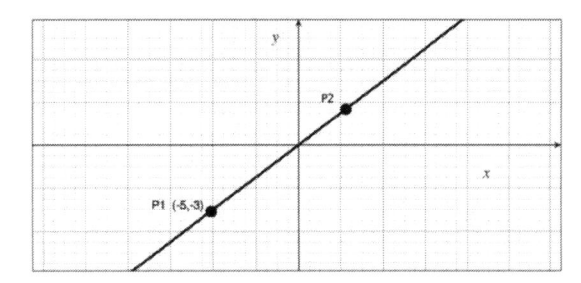

a. 0.8
b. 1
c. 5
d. 3
e. 8

40. What is the area of an isosceles triangle inscribed in a circle of radius r if the base of the triangle is the diameter of the circle?

a. r^2
b. $2r^2$
c. πr^2
d. $2\pi r$
e. $2\pi + 1$

41. A regular deck of cards has 52 cards. What is the probability of drawing three aces in a row?

a. 1 in 52
b. 1 in 156
c. 1 in 2000
d. 1 in 5525
e. 1 in 132600

42. If $ax^2 + by = 0$, which of the following must be true?

a. $ax^2 = by$
b. $ax^2 = \sqrt{by}$
c. $ax = b\sqrt{y}$
d. $ax^2 = -by$
e. $ax = b\sqrt{y}$

43. In the graph shown below, what is the slope of a line through the origin that will intercept the line y = f(x) at a point where y = 2?

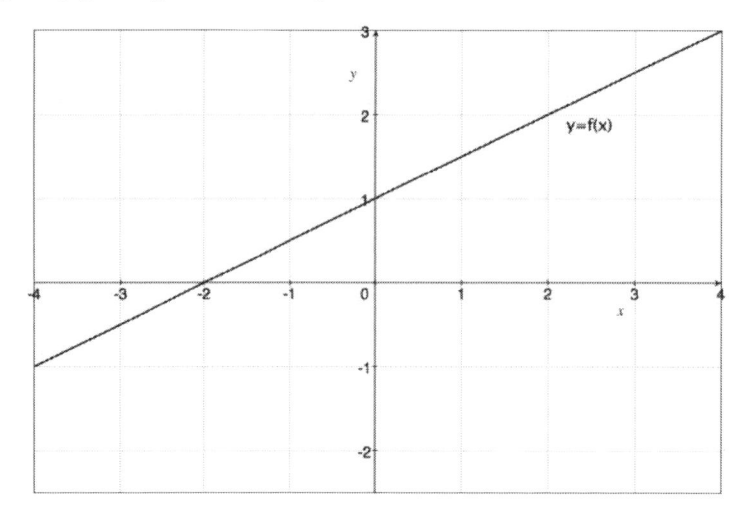

44. Equal numbers of dimes and pennies are placed in a single row on a table. Which of the following must be true?
   a. Every dime will be next to a penny.
   b. If there are two dimes at one end of the row, two pennies must be next to one another.
   c. If there is a dime at one end of the row, there must be a penny at the other end.
   d. Every penny will be between two dimes.
   e. If there are two pennies together anywhere in the row, there must be dimes at both ends.

45. A satellite in a circular orbit rotates around the Earth every 120 minutes. If the Earth's radius is 4000 miles at sea level, and the satellite's orbit is 400 miles above sea level, approximately what distance does the satellite travel in 40 minutes?
   a. 1400 miles
   b. 9210 miles
   c. 4400 miles
   d. 4120 miles
   e. 8000 miles

46. Which of the following equations best describes the straight line in the graph below? Note that a and b are non-zero constants.

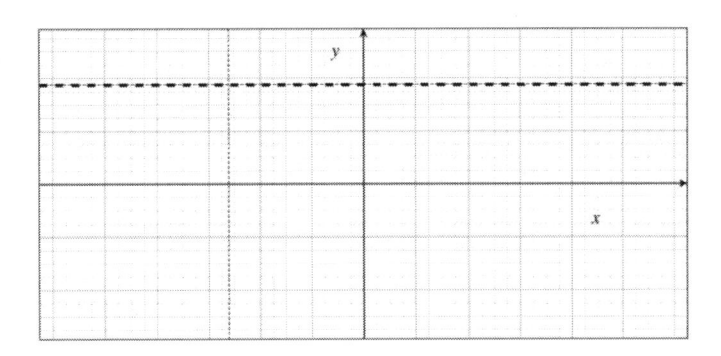

a. $y = x$
b. $x = a$
c. $y = ax + b$
d. $y = b$
e. $x = 0$

47. Determine which figure has a greater area: Figure A, which is a circle with a diameter of 9 inches, or Figure B, which is a circle with a radius of 5 inches.

48. A ticket agency finds that demand for tickets for a concert in a 25,000-seat stadium falls if the price is raised. The number of tickets sold, N, varies with the dollar price, p, according to the relationship $N = 25000 - 0.1p^2$. What is the lowest price at which they will sell no tickets at all?

a. $10
b. $25
c. $50
d. $500
e. $1000

49. Refer to the equation in Question 48, which gives the relationship between ticket price and number of tickets sold. No matter how many tickets are sold, the cost of putting on the concert is $500,000. Which of the following equations can be used to calculate the profit Q made for any ticket price?

a. $Q = 25{,}000p - 0.1p^3$
b. $Q = 25{,}000p - 0.1p^3 - 500{,}000$
c. $Q = 25{,}000p - 0.1p^3 - 500{,}000p$
d. $Q = p(25{,}000 - 0.1p) - 500{,}000$
e. $Q = p^2(25{,}000 - 0.1) - 500{,}000$

50. In the system of equations below, what is the value of y?

$$x^2 + y^2 = 24$$
$$2x^2 + 3y^2 = 52$$

Science

1. The rate of a chemical reaction depends on all of the following except
    a. temperature.
    b. surface area.
    c. presence of catalysts.
    d. amount of mass lost.

2. Which of the answer choices provided best defines the following statement?

For a given mass and constant temperature, an inverse relationship exists between the volume and pressure of a gas?
    a. Ideal Gas Law
    b. Boyle's Law
    c. Charles' Law
    d. Stefan-Boltzmann Law

3. Which of the following is exchanged between two or more atoms that undergo ionic bonding?
    a. Neutrons
    b. Transitory electrons
    c. Valence electrons
    d. Electrical charges

4. Which of the following statements is not true of most metals?
    a. They are good conductors of heat.
    b. They are gases at room temperature.
    c. They are ductile.
    d. They make up the majority of elements on the periodic table.

5. What is most likely the pH of a solution containing many hydroxide ions (OH-) and few hydrogen ions (H+)?
    a. 2
    b. 6
    c. 7
    d. 9

6. Which of the following cannot be found on the periodic table?
    a. Bromine
    b. Magnesium oxide
    c. Phosphorous
    d. Chlorine

7. Nora makes soup by adding some spices to a pot of boiling water and stirring the spices until completely dissolved. Next, she adds several chopped vegetables. What is the solute in her mixture?
    a. Water
    b. Vegetables
    c. Spices
    d. Heat

8. A cyclist is riding over a hill. At what point is his potential energy greatest?

   a. At the base of the hill
   b. Halfway up the hill
   c. At the very top of the hill
   d. On the way down the hill

9. Which of the following correctly describes the trait Ll, if "L" represents tallness and "l" represents shortness?

   a. Heterozygous genotype and tall phenotype
   b. Heterozygous phenotype and tall genotype
   c. Homozygous genotype and short phenotype
   d. Homozygous phenotype and short genotype

10. Which of the following waves is a type of electromagnetic wave?

   a. Ocean wave
   b. Sound wave
   c. Transverse wave
   d. Gamma wave

11. What law describes the electric force between two charged particles?

   a. Ohm's law
   b. Coulomb's law
   c. The Doppler effect
   d. Kirchhoff's current law

12. What process transfers thermal energy through matter directly from particle to particle?

   a. Convection
   b. Radiation
   c. Conduction
   d. Insulation

13. Which state of matter contains the least amount of kinetic energy?

   a. Solid
   b. Liquid
   c. Gas
   d. Plasma

14. Which of the following is true?

   a. Mass and weight are the same thing
   b. Mass is the quantity of matter an object has
   c. Mass equals twice the weight of an object
   d. Mass equals half the weight of an object

15. Which of the following is not a state of matter?

   a. Gas
   b. Liquid
   c. Lattice
   d. Solid

16. What is the name for substances that cannot be broken down into simpler types of matter?

   a. Electron
   b. Molecules
   c. Nuclei
   d. Elements

17. What are the two types of measurement important in science?

   a. Quantitative and numerical
   b. Qualitative and descriptive
   c. Numerical and scientific
   d. Quantitative and qualitative

18. What is the typical way a solid would turn to a liquid and then to a gas?

   a. Vaporization then melting
   b. Melting then freezing
   c. Vaporization then freezing
   d. Melting then vaporization

19. Which of the following correctly lists the cellular hierarchy from the simplest to the most complex structure?

   a. Tissue, cell, organ, organ system, organism
   b. Organism, organ system, organ, tissue, cell
   c. Organ system, organism, organ, tissue, cell
   d. Cell, tissue, organ, organ system, organism

20. If a cell is placed in a hypertonic solution, what will happen to the cell?

   a. It will swell.
   b. It will shrink.
   c. It will stay the same.
   d. It does not affect the cell.

21. What is the longest phase of the cell cycle?

   a. Mitosis
   b. Cytokinesis
   c. Interphase
   d. Metaphase

Use the following Punnett Square to answer questions 22 and 23:

B = alleles for brown eyes; g = alleles for green eyes

BB	Bg
Bg	gg

22. Which word describes the allele for green eyes?
   a. Dominant
   b. Recessive
   c. Homozygous
   d. Heterozygous

23. What is the possibility that the offspring produced will have brown eyes?
   a. 25%
   b. 50%
   c. 75%
   d. 100%

24. What are groups of cells that perform the same function called?
   a. Tissues
   b. Plastids
   c. Organs
   d. Molecules

25. When does the nuclear division of somatic cells take place during cellular reproduction?
   a. Meiosis
   b. Cytokinesis
   c. Interphase
   d. Mitosis

26. Which group of major parts and organs make up the immune system?
   a. Lymphatic system, spleen, tonsils, thymus, and bone marrow
   b. Brain, spinal cord, and nerve cells
   c. Heart, veins, arteries, and capillaries
   d. Nose, trachea, bronchial tubes, lungs, alveolus, and diaphragm

27. Which of the following statements correctly compares prokaryotic and eukaryotic cells?
   a. Prokaryotic cells have a true nucleus, eukaryotic cells do not.
   b. Both prokaryotic and eukaryotic cells have a membrane.
   c. Prokaryotic cells do not contain membrane-bound organelles, eukaryotic cells do.
   d. Prokaryotic cells are more complex than eukaryotic cells.

28. What is the role of ribosomes?

a. Make proteins
b. Waste removal
c. Transport
d. Storage

29. Which of the following is an example of a tissue?

a. Cortical bone
b. Liver
c. Mammal
d. Hamstring

30. The adrenal glands are part of the

a. immune system.
b. endocrine system.
c. emphatic system.
d. respiratory system.

31. Hemoglobin transports oxygen from the lungs to the rest of the body, making oxygen available for cell use. What is hemoglobin?

a. An enzyme
b. A protein
c. A lipid
d. An acid

32. Which of the following statements describes the function of smooth muscle tissue?

a. It contracts to force air into and out of the lungs.
b. It contracts to force air into and out of the stomach.
c. It contracts to support the spinal column.
d. It contracts to assist the stomach in the mechanical breakdown of food.

33. Which of the following sentences is true?

a. All organisms begin life as a single cell
b. All organisms begin life as multi-cellular
c. Some organisms begin life as a single cell and others as multi-cellular
d. None of the above

34. What are the two types of cellular transport?

a. Passive and diffusion
b. Diffusion and active
c. Active and passive
d. Kinetic and active

35. How many basic tissue types does a human have?

a. 4
b. 6
c. 12
d. 23

36. Which of the following terms means toward the front of the body?

   a. Superior
   b. Anterior
   c. Inferior
   d. Posterior

37. When both parents give offspring the same allele, the offspring is _____ for that trait.

   a. Heterozygous
   b. Homozygous
   c. Recessive
   d. Dominant

38. Which of the below is the best definition for the term circulation?

   a. The transport of oxygen and other nutrients to the tissues via the cardiovascular system
   b. The force exerted by blood against a unit area of the blood vessel walls
   c. The branching air passageways inside the lungs
   d. The process of breathing in

39. Which of the following is not a type of connective tissue?

   a. Smooth
   b. Cartilage
   c. Adipose tissue
   d. Blood tissue

40. How many organ systems are there in the human body?

   a. 4
   b. 7
   c. 11
   d. 13

Use the following passage and illustrations to answer questions 41-46:

> Pollutants typically enter seawater at point sources, such as sewage discharge pipes or factory waste outlets. Then, they may be spread over a wide area by wave action and currents. The rate of this dispersal depends upon a number of factors, including depth, temperature, and the speed of the currents. Chemical pollutants often attach themselves to small particles of sediment, so that studying the dispersal of sediment can help in understanding how pollution spreads.
>
> In a study of this type, a team of scientists lowered screened collection vessels to various depths to collect particles of different sizes. This gave them an idea of the size distribution of particles at each depth. Figure A shows the results for six different sites (ND, NS, MD, MS, SD, and SS). The particle size is plotted in phi units, which is a logarithmic scale used to measure grain sizes of sand and gravel. The 0 point of the scale is a grain size of 1 millimeter, and an increase of 1 in phi number corresponds to a decrease in grain size by a factor of ½, so that 1 phi unit is a grain size of 0.5 mm, 2 phi units is 0.25 mm, and so on; in the other direction, -1 phi unit corresponds to a grain size of 2 mm and -2 phi units to 4 mm.

Grains of different size are carried at different rates by the currents in the water. The study also measured current speed and direction, pressure and temperature at different depths, and at different times of year. The results were used in a computer modeling program to predict the total transport of sediments both along the shore (north-south) and perpendicular to it (east-west). Figure B shows the program's calculation of the distance particles would have been transported during the study period. The abbreviation mab in the figure stands for meters above bottom.

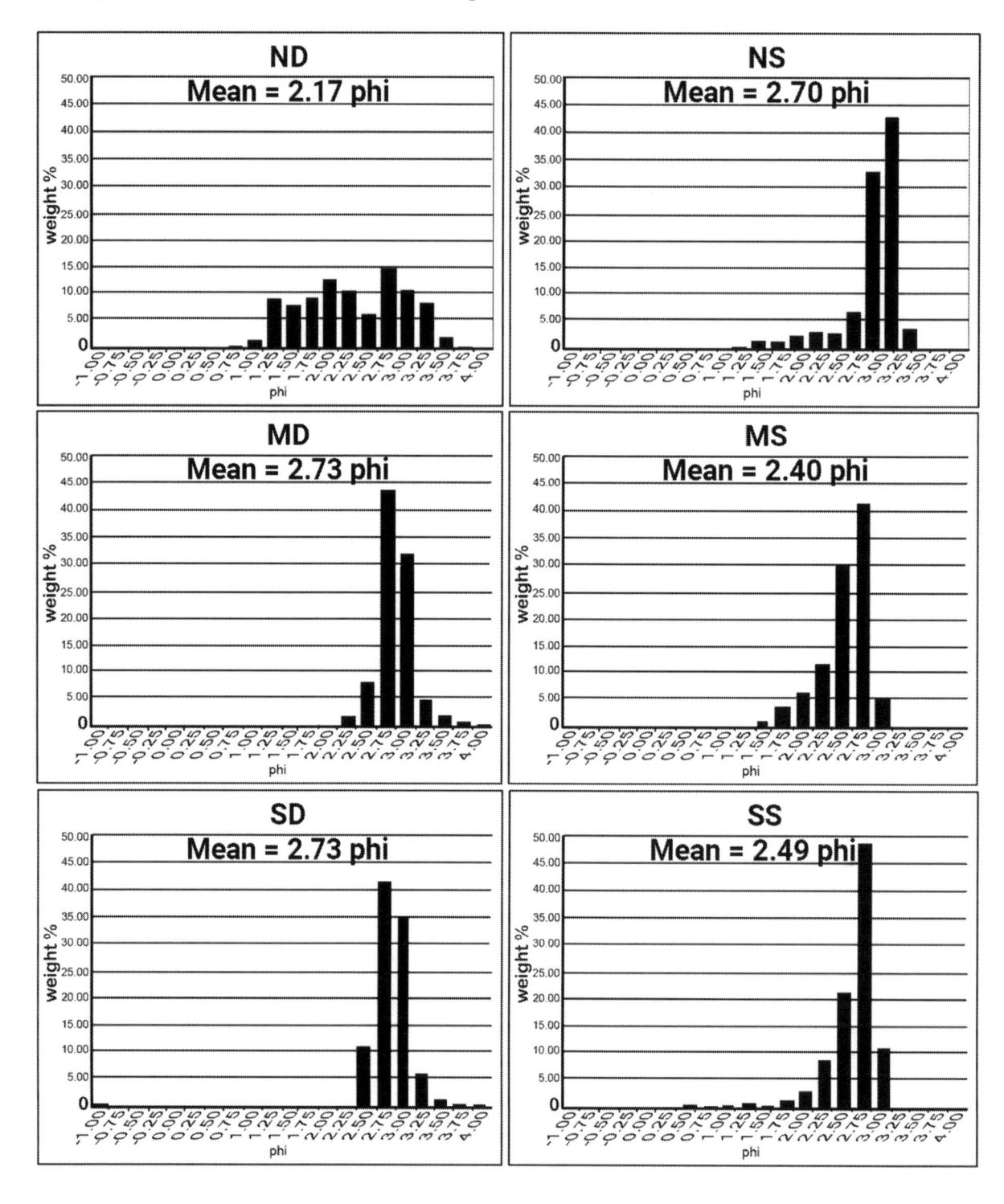

a) Cumulative Alongshore Transport

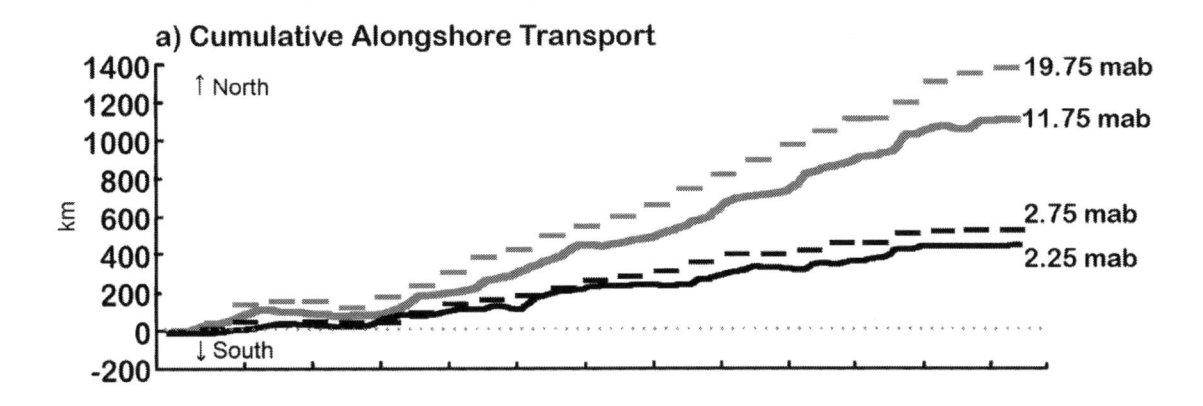

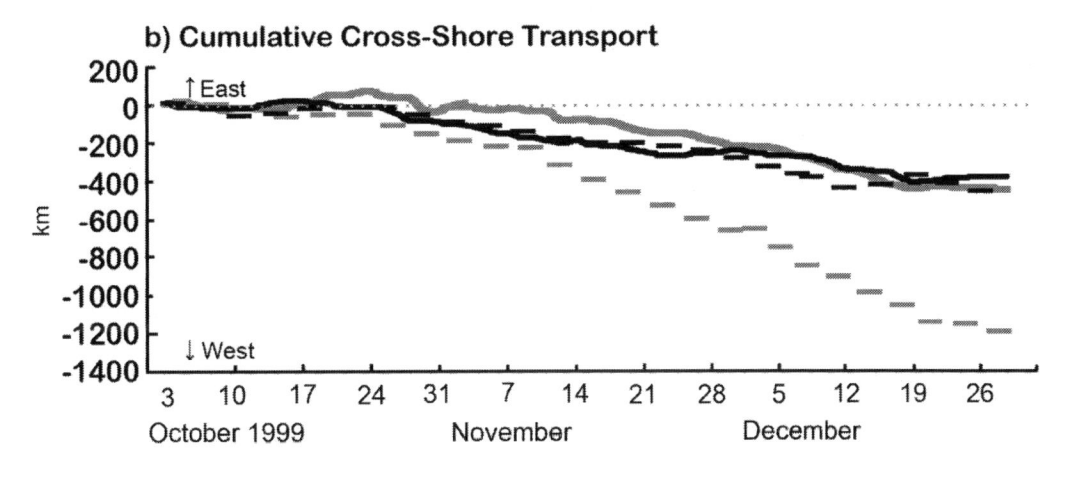

b) Cumulative Cross-Shore Transport

41. Which of the following sites was found to have the smallest average particle size?

a. ND
b. NS
c. MD
d. MS
e. SS

42. With the exception of a few outliers, all of the phi values were in the range 1.0 to 4.0. This means that

a. All particles studied were smaller than 0.5 mm.
b. All particles studied were between 1.0 and 4.0 mm.
c. No screens larger than 4.0 m were used in the study.
d. There were particle of all sizes in the study.
e. All particles were larger than 0.5 mm.

43. For which site is it least true that the mean particle size represents the entire population?

a. ND
b. NS
c. MD
d. MS
e. SS

44. What particle size corresponds to a phi value of -3?

a. 2mm
b. 0.5 mm
c. 0.0625 mm
d. 8 mm
e. 6 mm

45. In Figure B, the absolute value of the slope of the curves corresponds to

a. The speed of transport.
b. The size of the particles.
c. The phi value.
d. The depth.
e. The distance from shore.

46. The data indicates that along a NS axis

a. Transport is faster in deeper waters.
b. Transport is faster in shallower waters.
c. Transport is the same at all depths.
d. There is no correlation between transport speed and depth.
e. Transport is fastest at middle depths.

47. What does aerobic mean?

a. In the presence of oxygen
b. Calorie-burning
c. Heated
d. Anabolic

48. Scientists suggest that _____ has occurred through a process called _____.

a. evolution... differentiation
b. evolution... natural selection
c. natural selection... homeostasis
d. homeostasis... reproduction

49. Which of the following is not a product of respiration?

a. Carbon dioxide
b. Water
c. Glucose
d. ATP

50. Which of the following is an example of a non-communicable disease?

a. Influenza
b. Tuberculosis
c. Arthritis
d. Measles

Social Studies

HISTORY

1. Who became the commander of the Confederate army of northern Virginia at the beginning of the Civil War?

    a. Abraham Lincoln
    b. Thomas "Stonewall" Jackson
    c. Robert E. Lee
    d. Jefferson Davis

2. Which list is in the correct chronological order?

    a. Great Depression, Revolutionary War, first moon landing
    b. Revolutionary War, first moon landing, Great Depression
    c. First moon landing, Great Depression, Revolutionary War
    d. Revolutionary War, Great Depression, first moon landing

3. ARTICLE XXVII (Ratified July 1, 1971) of the United States Constitution states:

Section 1. The right of citizens of the United States, who are eighteen years of age or older, to vote shall not be denied or abridged by the United States or by any State on account of age.

This amendment to the Constitution was ratified in part because of what historical reality?

    a. Women gained the right to vote.
    b. Suffrage was extended to all African Americans.
    c. Young men were being drafted to serve in the Vietnam War.
    d. The number of people under 21 years of age increased.

4. Which country put the first satellite in space, in 1957?

    a. Russia
    b. United States
    c. Germany
    d. Korea

5. In 2002, President George W. Bush cited certain countries as being part of an "axis of evil." Which country was not part of that description?

    a. Iran
    b. Iraq
    c. North Korea
    d. Afghanistan

6. How did World War II influence American society?

    a. Consumption decreased in postwar American society.
    b. Thousands of people moved to find work in war-related factories.
    c. Racially integrated army units helped desegregate American society.
    d. Japanese-Americans were banned from serving in the U.S. military.

7. How did the Truman Doctrine shape U.S. foreign policy after World War II?
   a. It influenced President Truman's decision to create commissions on civil rights.
   b. It shaped the U.S. role in rebuilding the economies of postwar Europe.
   c. It led the U.S. government to refrain from interfering with the U.S. economy.
   d. It led to U.S. military involvement in countries such as Korea.

8. The United States fought North Vietnam in the 1960s and 1970s primarily to:
   a. spread democracy modeled on the U.S. system.
   b. demonstrate U.S. power to the Soviet Union.
   c. protect U.S. trade interests in Southeast Asia.
   d. prevent the spread of communism.

9. Which statement best describes the significance of the Mayflower Compact on colonial America?
   a. It declared that the colonists were independent from King James.
   b. It served as a blueprint for the later Bill of Rights.
   c. It provided the Pilgrims the first written basis for laws in the New World.
   d. It established Puritanism as the official religion for Puritan colonies.

10. Some American colonists reacted angrily to Great Britain's Navigation Acts in the seventeenth and eighteenth centuries primarily because
   a. the Acts restricted manufacturing in the colonies.
   b. the Acts forced the colonists to buy sugar from the French West Indies.
   c. the Acts gave the British a monopoly on tobacco.
   d. the Acts placed high taxes on the cost of shipping goods to Britain.

11. One of the earliest political parties in the United States was the Federalist Party. Its decline is best explained by:
   a. a failure to organize state political parties.
   b. the enmity of wealthy Americans.
   c. its opposition to the War of 1812.
   d. its advocacy of a strong central government.

12. Martin Luther King, Jr. and Malcolm X were both important figures in the American civil rights movement. Which of the following statements best describes a difference between their respective approaches to civil rights?
   a. Martin Luther King, Jr. advocated nonviolence; Malcolm X advocated self-defense against white aggression.
   b. Martin Luther King, Jr. mobilized ordinary citizens; Malcolm X focused on working with local white political leaders.
   c. Martin Luther King, Jr. related Christianity to civil rights; Malcolm X did not link religion to civil rights.
   d. Martin Luther King, Jr. promoted Black Nationalism; Malcolm X did not.

13. Which statement best describes how the 1944 passage of the G.I. Bill most influenced U.S. society?

a. It dramatically increased retention in the U.S. military.
b. It offered limited free housing for veterans.
c. It helped create a new middle class in U.S. society.
d. It transformed the work force by privileging veterans.

14. In 1973, the U.S. Congress passed the War Powers Act. How did the Act reassert congressional authority relative to that of the President?

a. It mandated congressional approval for funding war-related expenses.
b. It required the President to submit regular reports to Congress regarding conflicts lasting more than 60 days.
c. It restricted the power of the President to suspend key elements of the Constitution.
d. It limited the length of time the President could dispatch combat troops without congressional approval.

15. Which statement best describes how the 1896 U.S. Supreme Court decision in Plessy v. Ferguson most influenced U.S. society?

a. It reinforced the rights of individual states.
b. It legalized poll taxes and similar measures.
c. It provided a legal basis for racial segregation.
d. It determined the legality of railway strikes.

16. During the 15th century, Johann Gutenberg invented a printing press with moveable type. How did his invention influence science?

a. It did not influence science; the printing of Gutenberg Bibles directed public attention away from science and toward reforming the Catholic Church.
b. It led to scientific advances throughout Europe by spreading scientific knowledge.
c. It influenced scientific advancement in Germany only, where Gutenberg's press was based.
d. It did not influence science; though texts with scientific knowledge were printed, distribution of these texts was limited.

17. How did Eli Whitney's invention of the cotton gin in 1793 most influence the U.S. economy?

a. It elevated cotton as a basis of the Southern economy.
b. It led to many smaller cotton plantations.
c. It reduced the U.S. need to import cotton.
d. It decreased the dependence of plantations on slave labor.

18. Which is the best description of how Jonas Salk's 1955 development of the polio vaccine most affected American society?

a. The invention drastically reduced the incidence of polio in the United States.
b. The vaccine caused polio in some people who received the vaccine.
c. The announcement of the vaccine sparked a debate regarding the media and science.
d. The vaccine ignited a vigorous search for a cancer vaccine.

19. **Which of these presidents most greatly expanded the power of the presidency?**

    a. Thomas Jefferson
    b. Herbert Hoover
    c. Lyndon Johnson
    d. George W. Bush

20. **A nation that is NOT a member of NAFTA is:**

    a. Mexico.
    b. Brazil.
    c. the United States.
    d. Canada.

ECONOMICS

1. **India's economy can be best described as**

    a. a third-world country.
    b. one of the lowest producing economies in the world.
    c. a market-based system.
    d. an agricultural stronghold.

2. **Where is the U.S. banking system regulated?**

    a. On the local level
    b. On the state level
    c. On the federal level
    d. On both the state and the federal level

3. **What is the main way the U.S. government controls our money supply?**

    a. Changes in interest rates
    b. Raising taxes
    c. Striving for high economic growth
    d. Regulating inflation

4. **During which president's administration was Medicare and Medicaid started?**

    a. Lyndon Johnson
    b. Franklin Roosevelt
    c. Herbert Hoover
    d. Theodore Roosevelt

5. **Which factor is least likely to be considered to affect a country's gross domestic product (GDP)?**

    a. The size of its workforce
    b. The amount of its capital
    c. Technology in place
    d. Education of its workforce

6. **What does the Index of Coincident Indicators mainly measure?**

    a. The condition of the economy
    b. Housing starts
    c. Gross domestic product
    d. Changes in the business cycle

7. **What is the most likely result when the minimum wage is raised?**

   a. A decrease in saving
   b. A decrease in inflation
   c. An increase in saving
   d. An increase in inflation

8. **What is the most important component to a successful market economy?**

   a. Price
   b. Government
   c. Banks
   d. Demand

9. **Which statement best describes the difference between a monopoly and an oligopoly?**

   a. A monopoly involves a single supplier of a good or service; an oligopoly involves a small number of suppliers of a good or service.
   b. An oligopoly is a monopoly operating under price ceilings.
   c. In a monopoly, one company owns a single plant that produces a given good; in an oligopoly, one company owns several plants that produce a given good.
   d. An oligopoly is a legalized monopoly.

10. **Which combination of factors is most likely to cause inflation?**

    a. High unemployment and reduced production
    b. Credit restrictions and reduced production
    c. An oversupply of currency and a relatively low number of available goods
    d. An undersupply of currency and a relatively low number of available goods

CIVICS AND GOVERNMENT

1. **Which economic/political system has the following characteristics:**

   - private ownership of property
   - property and capital provides income for the owner
   - freedom to compete for economic gain
   - profit motive driving the economy.

   a. fascism
   b. capitalism
   c. communism
   d. Marxism

2. **Which of these would not be found in a democracy?**

   a. a congress
   b. a parliament
   c. a prime minister
   d. a dictator

3. An employer makes a rule that employees speak only English on the job. What law is this most likely to violate?

   a. Immigration Reform and Control Act
   b. Title VII
   c. Civil Rights Act of 1991
   d. Anti-Discrimination Act

4. Which freedom is not covered by the First Amendment to the Constitution?

   a. Freedom of the press
   b. Freedom from cruel and unusual punishment
   c. Freedom of assembly
   d. Freedom to petition the government

5. Which amendment guarantees a speedy trial in the United States?

   a. Fourth Amendment
   b. Sixth Amendment
   c. Eighth Amendment
   d. Fourteenth Amendment

6. What is the clearest way to describe a candidate who currently holds a political office?

   a. Incumbent
   b. Delegate
   c. Legislator
   d. Lame duck

7. How long is the elected term for a member of the Senate?

   a. 3 years
   b. 4 years
   c. 5 years
   d. 6 years

8. Which is not a constitutional responsibility of the president of the United States?

   a. Negotiating treaties with Senate approval
   b. Recommending legislation
   c. Choosing chairpersons for standing committees of Congress
   d. Seeking counsel of cabinet secretaries

9. Which government body has the least influence on foreign policy?

   a. Congress
   b. State Department
   c. Defense Department
   d. National Security Council

10. The U.S. government is best understood as a federalist government because:

    a. the legislative branch consists of two representative bodies.
    b. it is a representative democracy rather than a direct democracy.
    c. political power is divided between the federal government and the states.
    d. a national Constitution shapes national legislation.

11. How did isolationism most influence American society in the decade following World War I?

a. It shaped a temporarily strong economy as the U.S. avoided the troubled economies of postwar Europe.
b. It led to a system of admitting immigrants according to quotas based on their national origins.
c. It guided the U.S. government's decision to strengthen its navy as a safeguard against foreign attacks.
d. It influenced the collapse of trade deals, allowing U.S. companies access to oil in Colombia and in Middle Eastern countries.

12. The Seventeenth Amendment to the U.S. Constitution made the U.S. government more democratic by:

a. requiring state governors to be selected by popular election rather than by state electoral colleges.
b. mandating a regular national census to reevaluate state representation in the House of Representatives.
c. requiring U.S. senators to be selected by popular election rather than by state legislatures.
d. mandating regular state censuses to determine appropriate representation in state Houses of Representatives.

GEOGRAPHY

1. Iran, Iraq, and Kuwait all border what body of water?

a. Indian Ocean
b. Red Sea
c. Persian Gulf
d. Caspian Sea

2. The Andes Mountain Range is located on which continent?

a. North America
b. South America
c. Australia
d. Asia

3. Which of the following Roman numerals indicates the Colorado River in the figure below?
   a. I
   b. II
   c. III
   d. IV

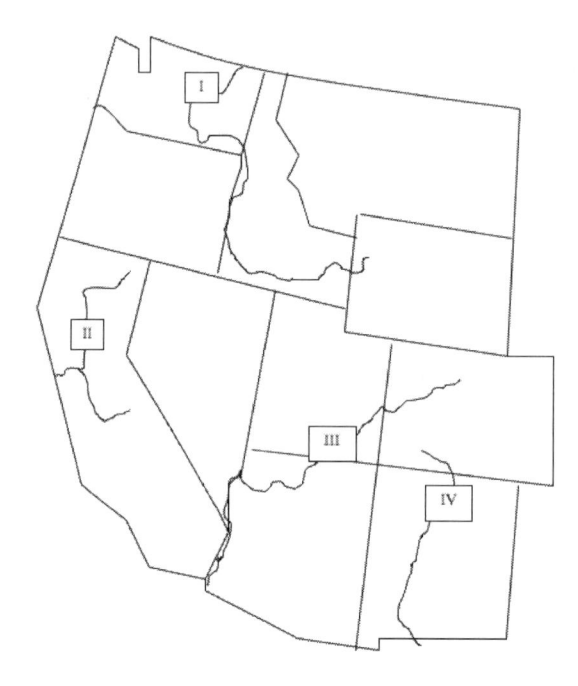

4. Which of the following resources in the West Bank is the most significant motivation for Israel's continuing occupation of that territory?
   a. The Mediterranean Sea
   b. Oil reserves
   c. Olive groves
   d. Aquifers

5. Consider the map below. Shaded areas indicate water use, with darker areas indicating heavier use. On the basis of the map, which of the following is the best inference regarding the areas where there is no shading?

    a. They are less inhabited.
    b. They are more desert-like.
    c. Residents are better at conservation.
    d. Residents require less water per capita.

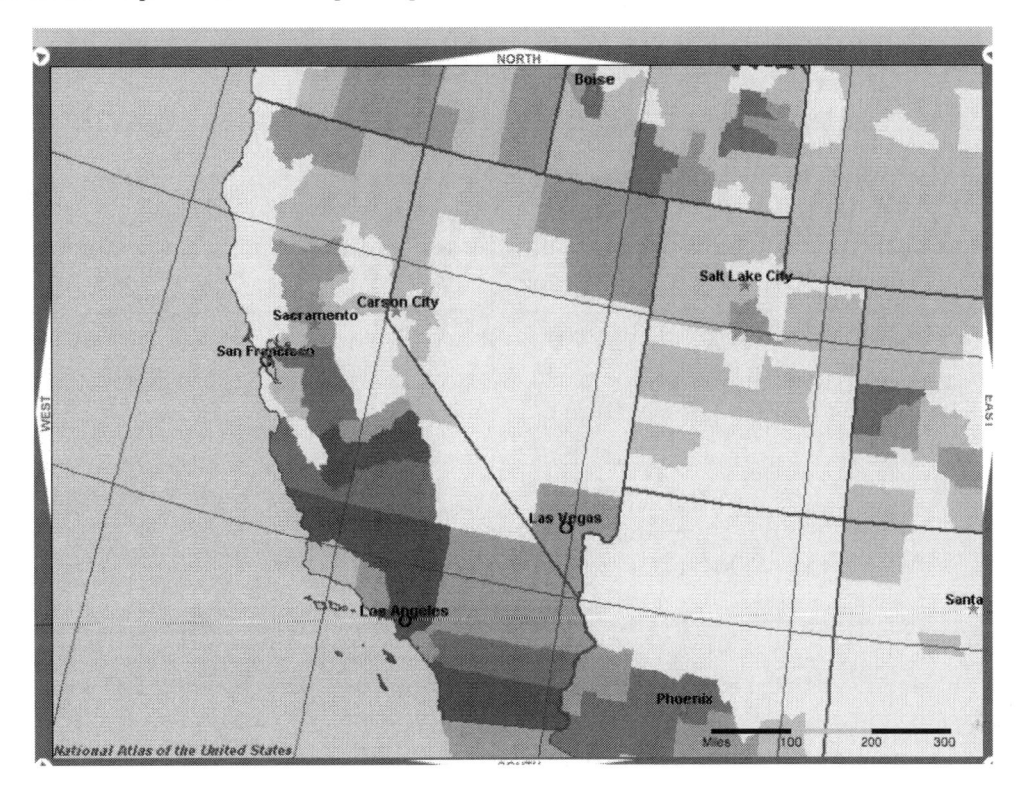

6. Which of these countries does NOT share a border with Israel?

    a. Jordan
    b. Saudi Arabia
    c. Lebanon
    d. Egypt

7. Which of these statements about Africa is true?

    a. It is nearly twice the size of the continental United States.
    b. It includes about 20 percent of the world's land surface but only 12 percent of its population.
    c. Almost the entire continent lies south of the equator.
    d. Nearly 50 percent of southern Africa consists of rain forest.

8. The physical geography of a region most directly affects:

    a. the religious beliefs of the native population.
    b. the family structure of the native population.
    c. the dietary preferences of the native population.
    d. the language spoken by the native population.

Answer Key and Explanations

Language Arts - Reading

1. C: Point of view refers to the vantage point from which a story is written. First person uses the pronoun *I*. Second person uses the pronoun *you*. Third person uses the pronouns *he/she/they*. There is no fourth person point of view. This passage was written in the third person.

2. B: The words "mysterious" and "important" used in the sentence help the reader deduce that Jo looked secretive. Jo neither looked jubilant, or joyful; disheveled, or disarrayed; or angry.

3. C: The last sentence states that Laurie was "an incorrigible tease." From this statement you can infer that Laurie was unruly or unmanageable. Stoic means not showing passion or emotion. Taciturn means silent. Uncanny means supernatural. There is nothing in the passage to imply he had any of these characteristics.

4. D: Personification is a metaphor in which a thing or abstraction is represented as a person. Personification is used throughout this poem. However, of the answer choices given, line 11 is the best choice. The author personifies spring as a female.

5. A: The fifth stanza gives clues to whom "we" refers.

> "Not one would mind, neither bird nor tree
> If mankind perished utterly"

"We" is referencing mankind.

6. B: This is an example of a rhymed verse poem. The last two words of each line rhymes in every stanza. A sonnet is a poem of fourteen lines following a set rhyme scheme and logical structure. Often, poets use iambic pentameter when writing sonnets. A free verse poem is written without using strict meter or rhyme. A lyric poem is a short poem that expresses personal feelings, which may or may not be set to music.

7. A: Answer choice A gives the best summary of the poem. The poem imagines nature reclaiming the earth after humanity has been wiped out by a war. The poet imagines how little the human race will be missed.

8. B: In the first paragraph of the essay, the author characterizes amateurs as "an elite group within the music scene" and states that there are several "technological, demographic, and economic factors" that account for them doing better than professionals. The tone of the essay is documentary—the author doesn't make any judgments about whether this is a good development or a bad one. He simply states that amateurs are more successful relative to professionals than they have been before and goes on to examine the reasons for this. Therefore, choice B is correct.

9. D: The key is the phrase "directly support." The essay needs to come right out and say the correct answer, not imply that it is true. Paragraph 3 says that digital file sharing "robs the professionals of what has traditionally been one of their biggest sources of revenue." Paragraph 2 provides less direct evidence, saying that many clubs that were once able to pay professionals now can't. Professionals have lost most of their income from both small clubs and recordings. Therefore, choice D is correct.

10. B: The second sentence in the final paragraph is a giveaway. If the "amateurs are the only ones who can afford to buy new gear and fix broken equipment, keep their cars in working order to get to shows, and pay to promote their shows," then the professionals must not be able to do any of those things, as stated in choice B.

11. C: The essay as a whole discusses how the current musical scene negatively affects professional musicians while leaving amateurs unharmed. The second paragraph, for example, discusses how professionals are no longer able to make a living playing small venues and must "fight more desperately than ever for those few lucrative gigs." The final paragraph states that, because of the effect on their finances, professionals are unable to maintain the gear and transportation they need to "keep the higher-paying gigs." It goes on to say that "a fairly skilled amateur . . . will be able to fake his way through most of what a professional does . . . to play professional shows." Therefore, professionals are falling behind amateurs at small venues (which professionals can't afford to play because of the lack of pay) and at professional gigs (where professionals can't play because they can't afford professional gear). Therefore, choice C is correct.

12. C

13. A

14. A

15. A

16. D

17. D

18. C

19. A

20. E: In the first paragraph, Miss Lucas states that "so very fine a young man, with family, fortune, every thing in his favour, should think highly of himself. If I may so express it, he has a *right* to be proud." Basically, she feels he deserves to be proud because he is physically attractive, comes from a good family, has money, and is successful. The best choice is (E).

21. A: This question is asking you to make an inference about Elizabeth's feeling towards the gentleman. In paragraph 2, Elizabeth is "mortified" by the gentleman's actions towards her. From this statement, you can make the inference that she was offended by his actions.

22. C: Theme is a message or lesson conveyed by a written text. The message is usually about life, society or human nature. This particular excerpt is exploring pride as it relates to human nature. Mary's observations on pride are the best summary of the theme of this passage. "By all that I have ever read, I am convinced that it is very common indeed, that human nature is particularly prone to it." The best answer choice is (C).

23. D: Paragraph 3 gives the answer to this question. According to Mary, pride is an opinion of yourself, and vanity is what we want others to think of us.

24. C: In the first sentence the phrase "so long had sleep been denied her" tells us she had been prevented from sleeping for some time.

25. D: The text tells us she was feigning, which means to pretend, to be asleep.

26. A: Despite his ugliness and deformity, Garth is a gentle soul who wants to be accepted as a friend by the girl.

27. E: AT first repelled by the sight of Garth in the window, the girl eventually expresses pity when she learns that he is deaf, too.

28. C: Garth's deformities are repugnant to her at first, and she must overcome this emotion.

29. B: He calls back to her that he is hidden from sight, and his voice is described as plaintive and pained.

30. B: The text tells us that he sees her lips move and assumes she is sending him away, because he cannot hear that she is calling to him.

31. D

32. D: At first, she was amazed at the extent of Garth's deformities, but she has quickly become more sympathetic and has come to pity him

33. E: The girl quickly understands Garth's sadness about his own condition and sympathizes with him.

34. C: Garth is sad that he is so deformed that other people are frequently repelled and try to avoid contact with him.

35. D: The girl has shown that she sympathizes with him by taking his arm, and Garth feels that he is being accepted despite his deformities.

36. C: The tricky thing about this question is that all the choices are true statements about things said in the essay. Only one, however, is the main idea. The best way to find it is to go to the first paragraph. In it, the author calls the ability to tell true and false statements apart "one of the main goals of every police officer." He goes further, calling this ability "the only way to punish the guilty, exonerate the innocent, and do the most possible good in preventing future crimes." Choice C, therefore, is the correct answer.

37. A: If there is one point that the author has repeated many times in this article, it is that police need to be able to investigate lies to conduct investigations. This is exactly the point explored in the explanation to question 33. Choice A is the correct answer.

38. C: In paragraph 2, the author states that "smoke" lies "slow down an investigation." Therefore, choice C is the correct response.

39. D: The work is important because "it is often viewed as the first significant work of English literature."

40. B: A supplier should reduce the price of a good if they want to sell more of it because, according to the passage, "consumers will demand less of a good if the price is higher *and more if it is lower.*"

Language Arts - Writing

1. A: The sentence, "Many people have proposed explanations for this drop," provides an introduction to the short explanations that follow. It should come after the first sentence.

2. B: The third sentence of this passage refers to "these insecticides," but there is no earlier reference to any insecticides in the paragraph. The sentence, "Insects that carry the disease can develop resistance to the chemicals, or insecticides, that are used to kill the mosquitoes," needs to be placed after sentence 2 for sentence 3 to make sense.

3. C: Sentence 4, regarding Jefferson's affair with one of his slaves, is not directly relevant to the main topic at hand, which is Jefferson's debts.

4. B: Sentence 2, regarding Feynman's musicianship, is of little relevance to the discussion of the atomic theory.

5. B: The part of the sentence "who says that..." is a parenthetical phrase about Richard Louv, not about the subject of the sentence. The "and who" is therefore incorrect, and the phrase needs to be set off from the sentence by a comma.

6. C: The best answer is (C) because it best captures the logical connection of the sentences: the fear of abduction is the *reason* parents are afraid to let kids play in the woods.

7. E: The sentence needs a subject. Answer (E) is the one that most clearly identifies a subject.

8. E: The "this" logically must refer to child abduction. Although not stated explicitly, it is the only choice that could logically be described as "a terrible thing" and "very rare."

9. B: Although the paragraph does not make its point explicitly, it clearly states that kids are spending too much time with video games and TV (being entertained by technology) and would be helped by more time getting their feet and hands dirty and touching things rather than just reading about them (having a +sensory experience of nature).

10. C: The adverb "particularly" clearly modifies the adjectival phrase "well known". Choices B and E subtly change the meaning. Choice D corrects the spelling of the original, but is a more awkward phrasing.

11. D: This eliminates the slang expression "what with". Choice E subtly changes the meaning.

12. B: Choices A and E awkwardly repeat the word "artist." Choice C fails to make the connection with the preceding sentence, establishing itself as the explanation for Daumier's lack of influence, and choice D fails to explain why other artists did not see Daumier's work.

13. B: Since the sentence begins with "This is also true," the phrase in choice B is redundant with the preceding sentence (see Question 32). None of the other choices address this.

14. A: This expands upon the previous sentence by explaining why he is considered the greatest sculptor of the era.

15. D: The word "however" shows that the sentence will provide a contrast to the preceding sentence. Choice B does this as well, but repeats the same expression used two sentences before.

16. C: The adverb "internationally" modifies the adjective "recognized." This answer has the best grammar and flow. Choice A has "internationally" incorrectly modifying "passports." Choice B misplaces the adverb "internationally" after the word "documents." Choice D has a singular pronoun modifying a plural noun. Choice E is missing the apostrophe after "bearers."

17. D: This choice has the necessary commas. Choice A is lacking commas after "grant" and "issue." Choice B needs an additional comma after "issue." Choice C incorrectly capitalizes "passports." Choice E does not pluralize "passport."

18. E: The sentences should be joined by a comma to make one sentence, which choice E does. Choice A is wrong because there are two sentences, but the "and" indicates a continuation of the idea. Choice B incorrectly uses a colon. A semicolon is used when there two independent ideas, which is not the case in choice C. Choice D incorrectly capitalizes the "A" in "and."

19. C: The sentence in choice C flows better that the other choices, and correctly uses a comma for an interrupter. Choice A does not flow. Choice B lacks the necessary comma. Choices D and E are both awkward.

20. B: This is correct because both "books" and "cards" should be plural. Choice A lacks the plural "cards." Choice C is incorrect because the verb "issue" is in the plural rather than the singular form. Choice D is incorrect because there is no reason for the word "use" to be in a possessive form. Choice E is incorrect because it places an unnecessary comma after "traditional."

21. C: Choice C is the best choice for the context. Choice B repeats sentence 8. Choices A, D and E, while true, don't provide any information that is pertinent to sentence 11.

22. D: There should be a comma after "November 30." Choice A is incorrect because the second sentence has no verb and is thus incomplete. Choice B incorrectly places a comma after "season." Choice C uses a semicolon incorrectly. Choice E does not need a comma after "runs."

23. B: The beginning of the sentence is in the present tense, so the verb in the second part of the sentence should be "includes." Choices A and D are wrong because they both use verbs in the past tense. Choice C is incorrect because the verb is in the future tense. Choice E is incorrect because the verb is a participle.

24. A: This choice is punctuated correctly. Choice B is incorrect because the order of information does not flow in the sentence. Choice C uses a semicolon incorrectly. Choice D places a comma is the wrong place. Choice E uses a colon incorrectly.

25. C: This is correct because it adds information similar to the theme of the passage. Choice B was already stated in sentence 4. Choice D basically says the same thing as sentence 9. Choices A and E are technically correct, but they do not follow the theme of the passage.

26. D: The preposition "when" indicates a relation of time. Choice A is not correct because there is no joining relation. Choice B is incorrect because it uses the wrong time relation. Choices C and E respectively indicate direction and choice, neither of which are time relations.

27. B: Choice A incorrectly places the primary thought of the sentence second. Choice C is awkwardly written and lacks a comma after the first "hurricanes." Choice D uses the incorrect verb form "includes." And choice E incorrectly makes the sentence into two sentences.

28. A: Choice B incorrectly uses a comma after the parenthesis. Choice C uses an apostrophe with "ghosts" where it is unnecessary because it is not a possessive form. Choice D uses a singular "hobgoblin" when it should be plural with all the other items in the list. Choice E puts a comma after "Halloween" where none is needed.

29. C: "Celtic Festival of Samhain" is a title, and so all the key words should be capitalized. Choice A is incorrect because "Festival" is not capitalized. Choice B incorrectly places a comma after "back." Choice D has an incorrect form of the verb "date," using a plural when the subject is singular. Choice E is also incorrect because it does not capitalize "festival" and uses a comma incorrectly after "thousands."

30. C: Choice A is not correct because sentence 4 is incomplete. Choice B is wrong because there are unnecessary commas after "souls" and "year." Choice D is incorrect because sentence 4 is not a complete sentence and the comma after "Because" is unneeded. And in choice E, the present tense "travel" does not agree with the past tense verb "had died."

31. E: "Over the years" is an introductory phrase and needs to be set off by a comma, so choice A is incorrect. Choice B incorrectly places a comma after "customs." Choice C is incorrect because the comma after "changed" does not belong there. Choice D is wrong because "Halloween" is not capitalized.

32. C: Choice C correctly uses a comma after "trick or treat." Choice A is not correct because there is no comma after "trick or treat." Choice B is not the correct choice because it does not have quotation marks around "trick or treat" to identify what the children are calling out. Choice D is incorrect because it uses the wrong tense of "fill." Choice E incorrectly places a comma after "doors."

33. D: Choice D correctly uses the pronoun "who," which agrees with "adults." Choices A and B respectively use the incorrect pronouns "that" and "which." Choice C is not correct because a comma would be needed after the opening phrase "just as much as children." Choice E incorrectly uses a comma after "adults."

34. C: Choice C makes sense in terms of the statement. Choices A and B suggest an opposite relationship, which does not fit in with the first sentence. Choices D and E are also incorrect.

35. A: The ideas in choice A follow logically. Choice B is awkward. Choices C, D and E do not make sense.

36. C: By adding the preposition "into" in choice C, the sentence makes sense. Choice A is not correct because it does not use a preposition. Choice B incorrectly uses the word "pressures." Choice D has the correct preposition, but it is missing the "will" of the contraction. Choice E is not correct because the word "hasty" does not require the article "an" in front of it.

37. E: The main idea is "shop," so putting it at the beginning of the sentence makes it flow the best. Choice A puts it at the end, which dilutes its importance. Choice B has incorrect use of commas before and after "shop around." Choice C would require a comma after "showrooms" to make it correct. Choice D is awkward and does not read well.

38. B: This choice conveys the correct meaning of the sentence. Choice A uses singular "service," when plural is needed. Choice C uses the word "contract" Instead of "contact." Choice D incorrectly places commas after both of the words "services." Choice E has the contraction "You'll" together with "may." There can be one or the other, but not both.

39. C: This choice places the comma correctly between "margin" and "which." Choice A needs a comma before "which." Choices B and D make no sense, and choice E is awkwardly worded.

40. C: By putting the secondary idea of a monthly payment in brackets, thereby omitting the "and" from the sentence and using a pronoun, the sentence reads very well. Choices A, B and D use dashes, commas, or a combination of the two, all of which result in poor readability. Choice E incorrectly uses a semicolon.

41. B: This choice is correct because it replaces the incorrect adverb "possibly" with the correct adjective "possible." Choice A incorrectly uses the adverb "possibly." Choice C uses the correct adjective, but the verb "can" does not go with the sense of possibility because it is too definite. Choice D incorrectly uses the conjunction "then" instead of "so," which indicates "as a result." Choice E is incorrect because the article "a" is not placed before the noun "possibility."

42. C: This choice is correct because it uses the preposition "with," which indicates "as a result." Choice A incorrectly uses the preposition "from," which indicates a starting place. Choice B uses the incorrect prepositions "with" and "within." Choice D uses the incorrect preposition "besides." Choice E incorrectly uses "then," which indicates "next" rather than a possibility.

43. A: This choice uses the correct verb form. Choices B, C and D all use incorrect forms of the verb. Choice E uses the correct verb form but it also uses a double negative, making it incorrect as well.

44. D: This choice uses a singular verb that agrees with the subject. Choice A is not correct because the plural verb does not agree with the singular "bank." Choice B incorrectly uses a semicolon after "services." Choice C uses the wrong preposition "within." And Choice E is incorrect because it uses "it's," the contraction of "it is," which is not needed here.

45. B: The verb "might be" indicates a probability. Choice A is not correct since the verb "must be" means something is necessary and has to be done, which is not the case here. Choice C is awkwardly written. In Choice D, the verb "have chosen" does not agree with the verb tense of the earlier verb "might be." Choice E is incorrect because it uses an incorrect comparative form of the adjective "good."

46. A: This choice is correct because it uses "In both cases" at the beginning, rather than at the end as choice B does. Choice C incorrectly uses the adverb "then" instead of the preposition "than." Choice D incorrectly capitalizes "Dollars." And choice E incorrectly uses the adjective "any" when the previous sentences have two subjects.

47. A: Choice A is the only option with the correct verb form. Choice B uses a plural verb form rather than a singular. Choice C has a verb in a past tense, when the "now" makes it clear that the sentence is in the present tense. Choices D and E both have incorrect verb forms as well.

48. A: Choice A uses the possessive of "service's" correctly. Choice B does not have a possessive. Choice C has no possessive and also has an incorrect verb form. Choice D uses an incorrect possessive form and choice E has a plural noun "milestones" with a singular article "a."

49. D: Choice A does not have "legacy" capitalized as it should be. Choice B does not have the proper name "forest legacy" capitalized. Choice C incorrectly capitalizes "the" and does not capitalize "legacy." Choice E does not capitalize "forest," which should be capitalized because it is a part of a proper name.

50. B: Choice B has a logical flow of ideas. Choices A, C, D and E are all awkwardly written.

Mathematics

1. C: To determine this, you must solve the given equation for x. Since $10x + 2 = 7$, we have $x = \frac{7-2}{10} = \frac{5}{10} = 0.5$, and $2x = 1$. Alternately, $10x = 5$; divide both sides by 5 to get $2x = 1$.

2. B: If the first lap takes 50 seconds, the second one takes 20% more, or $T_2 = 1.2 \times T_2 = 1.2 \times 60 = 72$ seconds, where T_1 and T_2 are the times required for the first and second laps, respectively. Similarly, $T_3 = 1.2 \times T_2 = 1.2 \times 60 = 72$ seconds, the time required for the third lap. Add the times for the three laps: 50 + 60 + 72 = 182.

3. B: Zero is the only number that gives the same result when multiplied or divided by a factor. In each case, the answer is zero.

4. B: The easiest pair to test is the third: $y = 4$ and $x = 0$. Substitute these values in each of the given equations and evaluate. Choice B gives 4 = 0 + 4, which is a true statement. None of the other answer choices is correct this number set.

5. E: The stock first increased by 10%, that is, by $10 (10% of $100) to $110 per share. Then, the price decreased by $11 (10% of $110) so that the sale price was $110-$11 = $99 per share, and the sale price for 50 shares was 99 x $50 = $4950.

6. D: The sides of a triangle must all be greater than zero. The sum of the lengths of the two shorter sides must be greater than the length of the third side. Since we are looking for the minimum value of the perimeter, assume the longer of the two given sides, which is 6, is the longest side of the triangle. Then the third side must be greater than 6 – 4 = 2. Since we are told the sides are all integral numbers, the last side must be 3 units in length. Thus, the minimum length for the perimeter is 4+6+3 = 13 units.

7. C: If $70, the amount used to buy more lemons, represents 35% of Herbert's earnings, then 1% corresponds to $\frac{\$70}{35} = \$2$, and 15% corresponds to $2 X 15 = $30.

8. C: She has been working at the rate of 10 papers per hour. She has 30 papers remaining and must grade them in the 2.5 hours that she has left, which corresponds to a rate of 12 papers per hour. $\frac{12}{10} = 120\%$ of her previous rate, or 20% faster.

9. D: The ratio of the ruler's height to the distance from eye to ruler, which is the tangent of the angle subtended at the eye by the ruler's height, must be the same as the ratio of the lighthouse's height to its distance, which is the tangent of the same angle. Since 3 inches is ¼ foot, we have $\frac{1/4}{2} = \frac{60}{D}$, and solving for D gives $D = \frac{2 \times 60}{1/4} = 4 \times 120 = 480$ feet.

10. E: $x^2 = 49$. When you take the square root of a number, the answer is the positive and negative values of the root. Therefore, $x = 7$ and $x = -7$. Only -7 is an answer choice.

11. The correct answer is 4.93. When gridding an answer that does not come out even, you must either enter the entire fraction, or as many decimal places as the answer field allows. The first two prime numbers larger than 10 are 11 and 13, and their product is 143. The largest prime number smaller than 30 is 29. The fraction will not fit in the answer field, so you must convert it to a decimal and round to the appropriate number of places: $\frac{143}{29} = 4.93$.

12. B: as the volume of a rectangular box can be determined using the formula $V = l * w * h$. This means that the volume of a rectangular box can be determined by multiplying the length of the base of the box by the width of the box and multiplying that product by the height of the box. Therefore, the volume of the box described in this question is equal to $5 * 7 * 9$, or 315 in³. (A) is incorrect because it provides the volume of a cylinder with a diameter of 9 inches and a height of 7 inches. (C) is incorrect because it provides the area of a rectangle with a base of 5 inches and a width of 9 inches. (D) is incorrect because it states the area of a rectangle with a base of 5 inches and a width of 7 inches, and (E) is incorrect because it states the *sum* of the length, width, and height rather than the *product* of length, width, and height.

13. C: If $5y - 20 < 0$, then $5y < 20$ and $y < 4$. Since y must be an integer, the answer must be 3, the largest integer that is less than 4. Choice B is wrong because, in this case, $5y - 20 = 0$, which is not less than 0.

14. The correct answer is 8. The total 20 + 13 = 33, but only 25 cars have been scored. Therefore 33 – 25, or 8 cars must have had both a man and a woman inside.

15. C: The line in the graph has a negative slope and a positive y-axis intercept, so the factor multiplying the variable *x*, or the slope, must be negative, and the constant, or *y*-intercept, must be positive.

16. The correct answer is 3. By definition, $x - 3 = 6$ and $x - 3 = -6$. Since x is defined as a negative integer, solve $x - 3 = -6 \Rightarrow x = -3$. The question asks for $|x|$, therefore $|x| = 3$.

17. B: The total volume of the cylinder is given by $V = h\pi r^2 = 10\pi \times 1 = 31.4$, when $\pi = 3.14$. Since the slice is a straight, 60-degree slice, its volume is one sixth of this $\left(\frac{60}{360} = \frac{1}{6}\right)$, or 5.23.

18. A: The median of a set of numbers is one for which the set contains an equal number of greater and lesser values. Besides Z, there are 8 numbers in the set, so that 4 must be greater and 4 lesser than Z. The 4 smallest values are 5, 7, 9, and 12. The 4 largest are 16, 18, 23, and 44. So Z must fall between 12 and 16.

19. C: If Q is divisible by both 7 and 2, it must be a multiple of 14, which is the least common multiple of both 2 and 7. Therefore, if one adds another multiple of 14 to Q, it will also be divisible by both 2 and 7. Of the choices given, only 28 is a multiple of 14.

20. The correct answer is 25. Three quarters of the fish, or 300, are red or blue, leaving only 100, or 25% brown fish. Since the probability of pulling out any single fish is the same, he has a 25% chance of getting a brown fish.

21. B: Simply substitute the given values for *a* and *b* and perform the required operations.

22. C: Every possible combination of scores is a multiple of 7, since the two terms of the ratio have a sum of seven.

23. E: To solve this problem, work backwards. That is, perform FOIL on each answer choice until you derive the original expression.

24. The correct answer is 21. The sentence in the question is translates to $3x - 5 = 58$. Therefore, $x = \frac{58+5}{3} = 21$.

25. A: A set of six numbers with an average of 4 must have a collective sum of 24. The two numbers that average 2 will add up to 4, so the remaining numbers must add up to 20. The average of these four numbers can be calculated: 20/4 = 5.

26. D: At the point of intersection, the y-coordinates are equal on both lines so that $2x + 3 = x - 5$. Solving for x, we have $x = -8$. Then, evaluating y with either equation yields $y = 2(-8) + 3 = -16 + 3 = -13$ or $y = -8 - 5 = -13$.

27. A: Evaluate as follows: $2f(x) - 3 = 2(2x^2 + 7) - 3 = 4x^2 + 14 - 3 = 4x^2 + 11$.

28. C: The hypotenuse must be the longest side of a right triangle, so it must be the lengths of the other two sides that are given as 6 and 8 units. Calculate the length of the hypotenuse, H, from the Pythagorean Theorem: $H^2 = S_1^2 + S_2^2 = 6^2 + 8^2 = 36 + 64 = 100$, which yields H = 10 and the perimeter equals 10+6+8 = 24.

29. C: This can be solved as two equations with two unknowns. Since the integers are consecutive with $p > n$, we have $p - n = 1$, so that $p = 1 + n$. Substituting this value into $p + n = 15$ gives $1 + 2n = 15$, or $n = \frac{14}{2} = 7$.

30. B: The square is one whose diagonal corresponds to the diameter of the circle. This allows calculation of the side a by the Pythagorean Theorem, where the diameter is $d = 2r$: $d^2 = 4r^2 = a^2 + a^2$. Thus, $4r^2 = 2a^2$, and the area of the square $a^2 = r^2$.

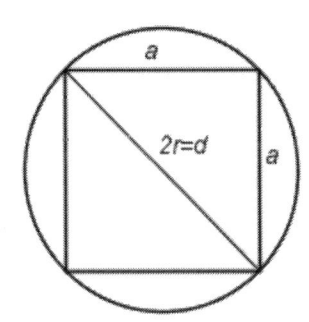

31. A: The mean, or average of the distribution can be computed by multiplying each grade by the number of students obtaining it, summing, and dividing by the total number of students. Here, n = 4.2. The median is the value for which an equal number of students have received higher or lower grades. Here, p = 4. The mode is the most frequently obtained grade, and here, q = 3.

32. D: Remember that when you multiply like bases, you add the exponents, and when you divide like bases, you subtract the exponents. $(xy)^{7y} - (xy)^y = (xy)^y[(xy)^{7y-y} - 1] = (xy)^y[(xy)^{6y} - 1]$

33. B: If the averages are equal, then we have $\frac{x+y+z}{3} = \frac{a+b+c}{3}$, so that it must be true that $(x + y + z) = (a + b + c)$. Therefore, the average of all six numbers is $\frac{(x+y+z)+(a+b+c)}{6} = \frac{2(x+y+z)}{6} = \frac{(x+y+z)}{3} = 23$.

34. The correct answer is 15. Subtracting the second equation from the first, we have $2x + y + 7a - 2x - y - 5a = 50 - 40$, which simplifies to 2a = 10, or a = 5. Substitute this value into either of the original equations. The first equation yields $2x + y + 35 = 50$, so that $2x + y = 15$. The second equation gives the same answer: $2x + y + 25 = 40 \Rightarrow 2x + y = 15$.

35. B: $(6a)x^2$ is equivalent to $6 \times ax^2$, so that ax^2 is simply 1/6th of this, or $\frac{30}{6} = 5$.

36. A: Since a player cannot remove fewer than 1 or more than 3 toothpicks per turn, it follows that leaving 2, 3 or 4 toothpicks in a row allows a winning response, and that leaving 5 toothpicks forces the next player to leave 2, 3, or 4.

37. The correct answer may be gridded as 24 in. The perimeter of a rectangle can be determined by using the formula P = 2 * (Side 1 + Side 2). This means that the perimeter of a rectangle can be determined by adding the length of the base of the rectangle to the height of the rectangle and multiplying by 2. Therefore, the perimeter of the rectangle described in this question is equal to 2 * (5 inches + 7 inches), or 24 inches. The other choices for this question are incorrect because they do not use the correct formula. (A) is incorrect because it simply offers the rectangle's height squared rather than using the appropriate formula. (B) is incorrect because it offers the area of the rectangle rather than the perimeter. (D) is incorrect because it offers the area of a triangle with a base of 5 inches and a height of 7 inches, and (E) is incorrect because it is simply the sum of the length and width.

38. E: The circular area covered by the sprinkler is πr^2, so the difference is obtained as $\pi \times 8^2 - \pi \times 6^2 = \pi(64 - 36) = 28\pi = 87.92$.

39. C: Since the line is straight, the slope is the same throughout. Thus, if 5 y-units are traversed in going from $x = -3$ to $x = 0$ (where y increases from -5 to 0, to reach the origin), then 5 y-units will be traversed in going from $x = 0$ to $x = 3$.

40. A: The area of a triangle equals half the product of base times height. Since the base passes through the center, we have base = 2 r and height = r, so that the area A is $A = \frac{r \times 2r}{2} = r^2$.

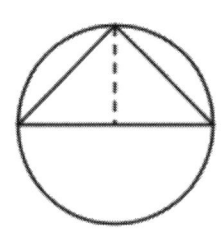

41. D: The probability of getting three aces in a row is the product of the probabilities for each draw. For the first ace, that is 4 in 52, since there are 4 aces in a deck of 52 cards. For the second, it is 3 in 51, since 3 aces and 51 cards remain; and for the third, it is 2 in 50. So, the overall probability, P, is $P = \frac{4}{52} \times \frac{3}{51} \times \frac{2}{50} = \frac{24}{132600} = \frac{1}{5525}$.

42. D: which is obtained by moving the second term to the right of the equality and changing its sign.

43. The correct answer is 1. At y = 2, we see that x = 2 for the plotted line. The equation for a straight line is of the form $y = ax + b$, where a is the slope and b is the y-intercept at x=0. If the new line passes through the origin, then b = 0, and the slope a must be 1 for y to equal 2 when x equals 2.

44. B: Since there are equal numbers of each coin in the row, if two of one type are next to each other, two of the other type must also be next to each other someplace within the row, or else at each end of the row. Since the two dimes take up one end of the row, the two pennies must be together.

45. B: The radius, R, of the satellite's orbit is the sum of the Earth's radius plus the satellite's orbital altitude, or R = 4400 miles. The circumference of the circular orbit is therefore $C = 2\pi r = 2\pi(4400 = 8800\pi$ miles. Since 40 minutes is one third of the satellite's 120-minute orbital time, it traverses one third of this distance in that time. So, the distance, $D = \frac{40}{120} \times 2\pi \times 4400 = 9210.66$ miles, using 3.14 for π.

46. D: The line in the graph has a constant value of y, one that does not change regardless of the value of x. This is a special case of the equation for the straight line, $y = mx + b$, for which m = 0.

47. The correct answer: Figure A has a greater area than figure B. A circle with a radius of 5 inches has a greater area than a circle with a diameter of 9 inches. This is because the area of a circle can be determined by using the formula A = π × r2 and the radius of a circle is equal to half of the circle's diameter. Applying these common geometric formulas to the problem, this means that the radius of figure A is 4.5 inches and the radius of figure B, which is stated within the question, is 5 inches. Therefore, the area of figure A is equal to 3.14 × 4.52 or 63.585 and the area of figure B is equal to 3.14 × 52 or 78.5.

48. D: When no tickets are sold, N = 0, and $0 = 25000 - 0.1p^2$, so that $0.1p^2 = 25000$, and $p^2 = \frac{25000}{0.1} 250,000 = 2500 \times 100 = 50^2 \times 10^2$, so that $p = 50 \times 10 = 500$.

49. B: Profit equals (tickets sold) x (price) – cost. The number of tickets sold is given by the equation in Question 12. Multiplying this expression by price, p, gives $25,000p - 0.1p^3$, and subtracting cost gives the expression in Choice B.

50. The correct answer is 2. Rearranging the first equation gives $x^2 = 24 - y^2$. Now, substituting this value into the second equation gives $2(24 - y^2) + 3y^2 = 52 \Rightarrow 48 - 2y^2 + 3y^2 = 52$. Rearranging once again gives $y^2 = 4$, or $y = \pm 2$. The grid does not allow for negative numbers, so grid in 2.

Science

1. D: The rate at which a chemical reaction occurs does not depend on the amount of mass lost, since the law of conservation of mass (or matter) states that in a chemical reaction there is no loss of mass.

2. B: Boyle's law states that for a constant mass and temperature, pressure and volume are related inversely to one another: PV = c, where c = constant.

3. C: An ionic bond forms when one atom donates an electron from its outer shell, called a valence electron, to another atom to form two oppositely charged atoms.

4. B: Metals are usually solids at room temperature, while nonmetals are usually gases at room temperature.

5. D: A solution that contains more hydroxide ions than hydrogen ions is a base, and bases have a pH greater than 7, so the only possible answer is D, 9.

6. B: Magnesium oxide cannot be found on the periodic table because it is a compound of two elements.

7. C: A solute is a substance that is dissolved in another substance. In this case, the solute is the spices

8. C: Potential energy is stored energy. At the top of the hill, the cyclist has the greatest amount of potential energy (and the least amount of kinetic energy) because his motion is decreased and he has the potential of motion in any direction.

9. A: The trait Ll describes the genotype of the person or the traits for the genes they carry. It is heterozygous because it contains a dominant gene and a recessive gene. Tallness is the phenotype of the person or the physical expression of the genes they carry, because L for tallness is the dominant gene.

10. D: Gamma waves are the smallest wavelengths of the electromagnetic spectrum.

11. B: Coulomb's law describes the electric force between two charged particles. It states that like charges repel and opposite charges attract, and the greater their distance, the less force they will exert on each other.

12. C: Conduction is the transfer of thermal energy between two substances that come into contact with each other; their particles must collide in order to transfer energy.

13. A: Solids contain the least amount of kinetic energy because they are made up of closely packed atoms or molecules that are locked in position and exhibit very little movement. Gases and plasmas exhibit the greatest amount of energy.

14. B: Mass is not the same as weight; rather, mass is the quantity of matter an object has.

15. C: There are three states of matter: gases, liquids, and solids.

16. D: An element is a substance that cannot be broken into simpler types of matter.

17. D: The two types of measurement important in science are quantitative (when a numerical result is used) and qualitative (when descriptions or qualities are reported).

18. D: A solid turns to a liquid by melting, and a liquid turns to a gas by vaporization.

19. D: The cellular hierarchy starts with the cell, the simplest structure, and progresses to organisms, the most complex structures.

20. B: A hypertonic solution is a solution with a higher particle concentration than in the cell, and consequently lower water content than in the cell. Water moves from the cell to the solution, causing the cell to experience water loss and shrink.

21. C: Interphase is the period when the DNA is replicated (or when the chromosomes are replicated) and is the longest part of the cell cycle.

22. B: Recessive alleles are represented by lower case letters, while dominant alleles are represented by upper case letters,

23. C: Dominant genes are always expressed when both alleles are dominant (BB) or when one is dominant and one is recessive (Bg). In this case, ¾ or 75% will have brown eyes.

24. A: Groups of cells that perform the same function are called tissues.

25. D: The nuclear division of somatic cells takes place during mitosis.

26. A: The immune system consists of the lymphatic system, spleen, tonsils, thymus and bone marrow.

27. C: Prokaryotic cells are simpler cells that do not have membrane-bound organelles, whereas eukaryotic cells have several membrane-bound organelles.

28. A: A ribosome is a structure of eukaryotic cells that makes proteins.

29. A: Cortical bone is a connective tissue acting as a hard part of bones as organs. A liver is an organ, a mammal is a type of organism, and a hamstring is a muscle.

30. B: The adrenal glands are part of the endocrine system. They sit on the kidneys and produce hormones that regulate salt and water balance and influence blood pressure and heart rate.

31. B: Hemoglobin is a type of protein found in the red blood cells of all mammals.

32. D: Smooth muscle tissue involuntarily contracts to assist the digestive tract by moving the stomach and helping with the breakdown of food.

33. A: All organisms begin life as a single cell.

34. C: The two types of cellular transport are active (which requires the cell to invest energy) and passive (which does not require the cell to expend energy).

35. A: There are four basic tissue types in humans: epithelial, connective, nervous and muscular.

36. B: Anterior means toward the front of the body.

37. B: When both parents give offspring the same allele, the offspring is homozygous for that particular trait.

38. A: Circulation is transporting oxygen and other nutrients to the tissues via the cardiovascular system.

39. A: Smooth is not a type of connective tissue. Cartilage, adipose tissue, and blood tissue all are.

40. C: There are 11 organ systems in the human body.

41. C: Of the sites listed, the phi value for site MD, 2.73 phi, is the largest value. The text explains how phi varies inversely with particle size, so these are the smallest particles.

42. E: According to the definition of phi supplied in the text, the range 1.0 to 4.0 phi units corresponds to particle sizes in the range 0.06 to 0.5 mm.

43. A: At all of the sites except site ND, the particle size distributions are tightly centered around a well-defined modal value. At site ND, the distribution is spread out over a broader range, and there is no well-defined central value.

44. D: Each unit of added phi value in the negative direction corresponds to a doubling of the particle size, so that -1 corresponds to 2mm, -2 to 4 mm, and -3 to 8 mm.

45. A: The curves represent the distance traveled, and they approximate a straight line. The slope of the line represents the speed of travel. Although the curve in part (b) has a negative slope, the absolute value of that slope will be a positive value, representing speed of transport towards the west.

46. B: The steepest slopes correspond to the greatest values of *mab*, or meters above bottom. These are the shallowest waters.

47. A: Aerobic means in the presence of oxygen.

48. B: Scientists suggest that evolution has occurred through a process called natural selection.

49. C: In respiration, food is used to produce energy as glucose and oxygen that react to produce carbon dioxide, water and ATP

50. C: Arthritis is a type of non-communicable disease because it is not passed from person to person.

Social Studies

HISTORY

1. C: Robert E. Lee declined Lincoln's offer to command the U.S. Army at the outbreak of the Civil War. He instead chose to become the commander of the Confederate army of northern Virginia. In the final phases of the war, he was the commander of all Confederate forces.

2. D: The correct order is Revolutionary War (1776–1783), Great Depression (1929), first moon landing (1969).

3. C: Young people protested being old enough to fight and die for their country while being denied voting rights. Choice A is incorrect because women had gained the right to vote with passage of the Nineteenth Amendment in 1920. Choice B is also wrong. African American males were guaranteed suffrage following the Civil War; African American females gained the right in 1920. The baby boom ended in 1964, so Choice D is not correct.

4. A: Germany developed rocket technology and the United States put a man on the moon in 1969.

5. D: In 2002, the United States was involved with nation building in Afghanistan.

6. B: Many Americans migrated during World War II, seeking work in war-related factories; boomtowns sprang up as a result. Some Japanese-Americans served in the United States military during World War II; in fact, the all-Japanese 442nd Regimental Combat Team, was decorated by the U.S. government for its service. This eliminates choice D. Answer C can be rejected because Caucasian and African-American soldiers served in segregated units. Answer A can be eliminated because consumption actually increased in postwar American society, as production was high and returning U.S. soldiers had income to spend.

7. D: The Truman Doctrine was intended to prevent Greece and Turkey from becoming communist countries. However, its broad language had implications beyond those two nations, suggesting that U.S. policy generally should be to aid people who resisted outside forces attempting to impose communist rule. This doctrine led to U.S. involvement in Korea and Vietnam, where U.S. forces fought against communist forces in those nations. The United States did have a plan for assisting the European economies, but it was the Marshall Plan, not the Truman Doctrine. This eliminates choice

B. While President Truman did establish a President's Committee on Civil Rights, it was not as a result of the Truman Doctrine. This eliminates answer A. Finally, when inflation plagued the postwar U.S. economy, the federal government took measures to address inflation and other economic issues, rather than steering clear of them. This eliminates choice C.

8. D: During the Vietnam War, a central aim of the United States was to prevent the spread of communism. At the time of the war, North Vietnamese communist forces threatened South Vietnam, and the United States came to the aid of the South Vietnamese government. The Domino Theory of communism held that one nation's conversion to communism was likely to lead to other nations in that region also converting to communism. The aim of the United States was essentially negative (to stop communism) rather than positive (to implement a specific kind of democracy). This eliminates option A. Option B and C can both be rejected because neither describes the primary aim of U.S. involvement in Vietnam in the 1960s and 1970s. While A, B, and C could have been incidental benefits obtained by fighting North Vietnam, none correctly state the primary goal of the U.S.

9. C: The male passengers of the Mayflower signed the Compact after a disagreement regarding where in the Americas they should establish a colony. The Compact served as a written basis for laws in their subsequent colony. Because the Mayflower Compact did not list particular rights, it is not best understood as a blueprint for the Bill of Rights. This eliminates choice B. Though the Compact did in part serve as a basis for government, it did not declare independence from King James; its last line, for example, specifically refers to King James as the writers' sovereign. This eliminates choice A. Finally, although the Mayflower Compact does include religious language, it is a brief document that does not detail, defend, or establish as official any particular religious doctrine, including Puritan religious doctrine. This eliminates choice D.

10. A: The Navigation Acts in the seventeenth and eighteenth centuries restricted commercial activity in the American colonies and resulted in the constraint of manufacturing. The Acts were a logical extension of British mercantilism, a view according to which the colonies existed primarily to benefit Great Britain. Answer B can be rejected because one Navigation Act forced the colonists to buy more expensive sugar from the British West Indies, rather than the French West Indies. Option C can be eliminated because a positive result of the Navigation Acts was giving the American colonists a monopoly on tobacco by restricting tobacco production in Great Britain itself. Option D can be eliminated because the Acts did not place a tax on shipping goods to Great Britain.

11. C: The Federalist Party advocated a pro-British foreign policy and therefore opposed the War of 1812. This made the Federalists unpopular with many Americans; this unpopularity deepened when the war ended with American victory. The Federalist Party did advocate a strong central government; however, this position was not a key factor in the Party's decline. This eliminates option D. Option A can be rejected because the Federalist Party did organize state political parties in states such as Connecticut, Delaware, and Maryland. Many members of the Federalist Party were pro-trade and pro-business, as many members were well-to-do businessmen. This eliminates option B.

12. A: While Martin Luther King is famous for his advocacy of nonviolence, Malcolm X defended self-defense against aggression by white people. In the course of his work, King did indeed mobilize ordinary citizens; however, Malcolm X did not focus on working with local white political leaders, but instead focused on black communities. This eliminates option B. Malcolm X also sometimes spoke against black citizens practicing Christianity, linking the practice of that religion in part to oppression; this eliminates option C. Finally, option D can be rejected because King did not promote Black Nationalism, while Malcolm X did.

13. C: The 1944 G.I. Bill offered several significant benefits for U.S. U.S. veterans. These included economic assistance for veterans to attend college, mortgage subsidies, and unemployment benefits. Over a million veterans took advantage of the opportunity to attend college, and many homes were built with support provided by the G.I. Bill. This increase in home ownership and the availability of higher education contributed to the creation of a new middle class. The Bill did not offer veterans specific incentives for staying in the military after World War II; this eliminates option A. It did not offer free housing for veterans; this eliminates option B. Finally the Bill did not privilege veterans in the work force; this eliminates option D.

14. D: Under the War Powers Act of 1973, the President can send combat troops to battle (or to an area where hostilities are imminent) for only 60 days, with the possibility of extending this period of time to 90 days. In order to keep deployed troops in place (or to send additional troops) after this period of time has elapsed, the President must seek Congressional approval, either in the form of a mandate or in the form of a declaration of war. Option A can be eliminated because Congress was responsible for approving war-related funding prior to the War Powers Act, which did not affect this responsibility. Neither option B nor option C accurately describes the importance of the War Powers Act.

15. C: The U.S. Supreme Court decision in Plessy v. Ferguson affirmed the state of Louisiana's constitutional right to offer "separate but equal" accommodations on railway lines within that state. The decision provided a legal basis for racial segregation in U.S. society, including segregation in education and other public services. Option A can be rejected because the primary importance of the ruling was less to reinforce state's rights than to affirm the supposed legality of segregation. The decision produced increasingly significant consequences as U.S. society continued to segregate. Plessy v. Ferguson did not address poll taxes or the legality of railway strikes; this eliminates options B and D.

16. B: Johann Gutenberg's printing press led to increased scientific knowledge and advancement as scientific texts were printed and dispersed throughout Europe. Because the distribution of such texts extended outside of Germany, options C and D may be eliminated. Gutenberg Bibles were printed using Gutenberg's press, and thus Gutenberg's invention was likely a factor in the Reformation of the Catholic Church. In fact, Martin Luther's Ninety-Five Theses (against the Catholic Church) were printed using a printing press. However, this reformation occurred alongside, rather than in place of, the advancement of scientific knowledge. This eliminates option A.

17. A: Eli Whitney's invention of the cotton gin, a mechanism for quickly separating cotton seeds from cotton fiber, helped elevate cotton as a basis of the Southern economy. Option B can be rejected because, rather than leading to smaller plantations, the invention led to larger cotton plantations. Choice C can be rejected because the United States did not need to import cotton; rather, particularly after the invention of the cotton gin, the United States became a leading exporter of cotton. Finally, option D can be rejected because with larger plantations came an increased need for slaves: the cotton gin had the effect of increasing dependence on slave labor rather than decreasing it.

18. A: Jonas Salk's polio vaccine prevented thousands of new cases of polio in a nation which had become accustomed to the ravages of the disease. The invention was a major innovation that affected Americans all over the United States, as children were vaccinated against the disease. Unfortunately, Salk's vaccine did cause polio in a small number of children; however, option B can be rejected because the impact of this was lesser than the impact than the near eradication of the disease in the United States. Option C can be rejected because, although Salk's manner of announcing the vaccine ruffled the feathers of some of his scientist peers, it did not ignite a widespread or public debate regarding the media and science. Finally, option D can be rejected because it is simply false.

19. C: Johnson exerted his presidential power to advance the Great Society agenda and to enact major civil rights legislation. He also conducted a war in Vietnam without Congressional declaration. Jefferson, Hoover, and Bush were all outspoken advocates of limiting the role of government, including the executive branch.

20. B: The North American Free Trade Agreement was established in 1994 by the United States, Canada, and Mexico in an effort to minimize trade barriers among the continent's three nations.

ECONOMICS

1. C: In recent years, India's economy has been shaping into a market-based economy. This is an economic system that relies on supply and demand to set prices, rather than having prices set by the government.

2. D: The U.S. banking system is one of the most regulated banking systems in the world, with regulations within each state and the federal government.

3. A: The Federal Reserve System raises and lowers the prime rate to regulate the nation's money supply.

4. A: Although many programs were introduced under Franklin Roosevelt's New Deal, the Medicaid and Medicare programs were started by Johnson.

5. D: The education of the workforce generally does not affect GDP. The size of the workforce implies that there are people who are ready and willing to work. The amount of capital means that there is a sufficient number of factories and assets available to create goods and services. Technology includes the skills and knowledge people have to direct and enable the workforce.

6. A: The Index has four different indicators to assess the country's economic growth.

7. D: Raising the minimum wage ultimately causes a rise in the rate of inflation, since employers' labor costs are raised. Employers pass this increase on as higher prices for their goods and services.

8. A: Price determines what goods will be produced, who will be producing them, and how they will be produced. Banks and demand are both affected by price. Government is not a big part of a market economy and is more a part of a command economy.

9. A: When a company has a monopoly, it is the sole supplier of a good or service and therefore exercises great control over the price of that good or service. In an oligopoly, a small number of companies supply a given good or service (these companies might also act to control prices of that good or service). Because a monopoly differs from an oligopoly in this fundamental way, options B and D can each be rejected, as those answers describe an oligopoly as a kind of monopoly. Also, a monopoly might involve only one plant, but it could just as easily involve more than one; the distinguishing feature of a monopoly is its control over supply, not the number of plants or factories it uses in production. This eliminates option C.

10. C: Inflation is an overall increase in prices. Inflation commonly occurs when there is a large amount of printed currency circulating in an economy at a time when there are few available goods relative to that amount. Options A and B can be eliminated because each describe conditions under which deflation occurs (an overall falling of prices, the opposite of inflation). Option D can be rejected because when there is a relatively low amount of currency circulating within in an economy together with a relatively low number of available goods, prices are not apt to rise.

CIVICS AND GOVERNMENT

1. B: These characteristics describe capitalism.

2. D: A dictator is a leader with absolute power without respect to constitutional limitations. This would not be found in a democracy. Democracy is rule by the people; government by the consent of the governed.

3. B: Title VII prohibits intentional discrimination and practices with the effect of discriminating against individuals because of their race, color, national origin, religion, or gender.

4. B: The First Amendment covers freedom of the press, petitioning the government, and assembling peacefully. "Cruel and unusual punishment" is covered in the Eighth Amendment.

5. B: The Fourth Amendment outlaws unreasonable search and seizure. The Eighth Amendment protects against excessive bail. The Fourteenth Amendment states the rights of citizenship.

6. A: A delegate is a person chosen to serve on a particular committee or group. A legislator is a lawmaker. A lame duck is a person who is holding an office but will not retain it.

7. D: Senators are elected for a term of 6 years.

8. C: Chairpersons for standing committees of Congress are chosen by leaders of the majority party.

9. A: Although Congress must agree to pay for foreign policy dictated by the president, it does not decide foreign policy.

10. C: A federalist system of government is a government under which power is shared by a central authority and sub-components of the federation. In the United States in particular, power is shared by the federal government and the individual states. Option A, that the legislative branch consists of two representative bodies (the House of Representatives and the Senate) is true, of course, but does not describe a uniquely federalist structure. Rather, it describes the concept of bicameralism. Option A may thus be eliminated. Option B, likewise, describes different types of democracy but not federalism. B can thus be eliminated. Regarding option D, this statement is also true (the U.S. Constitution shapes national legislation) but it is not a descriptive statement of the federalist system because the statement makes no mention that power is shared by the states.

11. B: After World War I, the United States passed the Immigration Act of 1924, which regulated the number of immigrants in part according to their national origin. The United States sought to avoid the problems of Europe and other nations by limiting the number of foreigners who entered the United States. Option A can be rejected because quite soon after World War I, both inflation and unemployment were significant problems in the United States. Option C can be rejected because in the years immediately following World War I, the United States did not built its navy even to the extent allowed by treaty. Finally, option D can be rejected because after World War I, the United States made arrangements for the U.S. to have access to oil in Colombia and in Middle Eastern countries.

12. C: Prior to the Seventeenth Amendment, adopted in 1913, U.S. senators were chosen by state legislatures rather than by popular state elections. The former system caused problems beginning in the mid-nineteenth century, problems exacerbated by the fact that there was no consistent process among the states for just how state legislatures chose their U.S. Senators. The Seventeenth Amendment required that U.S. Senators be chosen by direct popular election by the citizens of the relevant state. The Seventeenth Amendment did not concern state senators (i.e., senators serving state Senates), governors, or censuses to determine the appropriate level of representation in a House of Representatives. This eliminates options A, B, and D.

GEOGRAPHY

1. C: Iran, Iraq, and Kuwait all border the Persian Gulf.

2. B: The Andes mountain range is the world's longest continental mountain range. It lies as a continuous chain of mountains along the western coast of South America.

3. C: Roman numeral III indicates the Colorado River. The Colorado River begins in Colorado and journeys through Arizona, Utah, and Nevada along the border of California, and into Mexico. The Colorado River is a major river; it is responsible for carving out the Grand Canyon, and is important for agricultural use and other uses. Roman numeral I indicates the Snake River. Roman numeral II indicates the Sacramento River. Roman numeral IV indicates the Rio Grande River. Each of these rivers is a major river in the United States, but all are separate bodies of water from the Colorado River.

4. D: The West Bank contains a number of significant natural water reserves (aquifers). These aquifers are an important source of water not only to the Palestinians living in the West Bank but to Israel as well. Access to these aquifers is a significant motivation to Israel's continuing control of the West Bank. The West Bank does not border the Mediterranean Sea; this eliminates option A. There are no significant oil reserves in the West Bank; this eliminates option B. Though there are olive groves in the West Bank, olives and olive products are far less important resources to Israel than water.

5. A: the most reasonable inference based on the data given by the map is that the areas with no shading (which represent areas of low water use) are less inhabited than areas with shading. Note that the areas with no shading also have no listed cities; cities on the map are surrounded by shaded areas. Because the map does not give any information regarding how much water is required per capita, option D can be rejected. The map gives no indication regarding residents' prowess at conservation efforts (positive or negative). This eliminates option C. Additionally, there is no indication from the map that any land is more desert-like. In fact, some of the lightly-shaded are is adjacent to the ocean. Therefore, option B can be rejected.

6. B: Although both Israel and Saudi Arabia border on the Gulf of Aqaba, Jordan stands between Israel and its giant neighbor to the southeast.

7. B: Three times the size of the continental United States, Africa contains a surprisingly small percentage of the world population. The continent is divided roughly in half by the equator. The rain forest makes up about 15 percent of central Africa.

8. C: Physical geography focuses on processes and patterns in the natural environment. What people eat in any given geographic region is largely dependent on such environmental factors as climate and the availability of arable land. Religion, family, and language may all be affected by geographical factors, but they are not as immediately affected as dietary preferences.

Practice Test #2

Language Arts - Reading

Questions 1-5 refer to the following passage:

There will come soft rains and the smell of the ground,

And swallows circling with their shimmering sound;

And frogs in the pools singing at night,

And wild plum trees in tremulous white;

Robins will wear their feathery fire

Whistling their whims on a low fence-wire;

And not one will know of the war, not one

Will care at last when it is done.

Not one would mind, neither bird nor tree

If mankind perished utterly;

And Spring herself, when she woke at dawn,

Would scarcely know that we were gone.

1. **How many stanzas does this poem have?**
    a. 2
    b. 4
    c. 6
    d. 10
    e. 12

2. **Which line uses personification?**
    a. Line 2
    b. Line 4
    c. Line 7
    d. Line 10
    e. Line 11

3. **The "we" used in line 12 refers to**
    a. all of mankind.
    b. the victors of the war.
    c. Americans.
    d. the poet and the reader.
    e. the animals.

4. **This poem is an example of a(n)**
   a. sonnet.
   b. rhymed verse.
   c. free verse.
   d. lyric.
   e. epic.

5. **Which of these statements offers the best summary of the poem?**
   a. Nature does not care about the affairs of mankind.
   b. It is the government's responsibility to fight a war.
   c. War has a devastating impact on nature.
   d. Wars should not be fought in the spring.
   e. Robins will sing about the war.

Questions 6-11 refer to the following passage:

George Washington Carver was always interested in plants. When he was a child, he was known as the "plant doctor." He had a secret garden where he grew all kinds of plants. People would ask him for advice when they had sick plants. Sometimes he'd take their plants to his garden and nurse them back to health.

Later, when he was teaching at Tuskegee Institute, he put his plant skills to good use. Many people in the South had been growing only cotton on their land. Cotton plants use most of the nutrients in the soil. (Nutrients provide nourishment to plants.) So the soil becomes "worn out" after a few years. Eventually, cotton will no longer grow on this land.

This was especially bad for poor African American farmers, who relied on selling cotton to support themselves. Carver was dedicated to helping those farmers, so he came up with a plan.

Carver knew that certain plants put nutrients back into the soil. One of those plants is the peanut! Peanuts are also a source of protein.

Carver thought that if those farmers planted peanuts, the plants would help restore their soil, provide food for their animals, and provide protein for their families--quite a plant! In 1896 peanuts were not even recognized as a crop in the United States, but Carver would help change that.

Carver told farmers to rotate their crops: plant cotton one year, then the next year plant peanuts and other soil-restoring plants, like peas and sweet potatoes. It worked! The peanut plants grew and produced lots of peanuts. The plants added enough nutrients to the soil so cotton grew the next year.

6. **Why was George Washington Carver known as the "plant doctor"?**
   a. He studied medicine in college.
   b. He grew peanuts on sick soil.
   c. He was a plant pathologist.
   d. He could nurse sick plants back to health.
   e. He knew plants could put nutrients back into the soil.

7. **How is this passage structured?**
    a. cause and effect
    b. problem and solution
    c. chronological order
    d. compare and contrast
    e. proposition and support

8. **According to the passage, what problem were cotton farmers facing?**
    a. They needed food for their animals.
    b. Peanuts were not recognized as a crop in the United States.
    c. They were growing too much cotton.
    d. Tuskegee Institute needed more teachers.
    e. The cotton had stripped the land of its nutrients.

9. **How did Carver resolve the farmers' problem?**
    a. He told the farmers to rotate their crops.
    b. He came up with a plan.
    c. He invented the peanut.
    d. He gave advice to farmers with sick plants.
    e. He provided protein for the farmers' families.

10. **This passage is mainly about**
    a. how George Washington Carver invented the cotton gin.
    b. how George Washington Carver became a teacher at the Tuskegee Institute.
    c. how George Washington Carver helped farmers improve their crop   production.
    d. why George Washington Carver studied plants.
    e. how George Washington Carver made peanuts a recognized crop in the   United States.

11. **According to this passage, "crop rotation" can be described as**
    a. planting a soil depleting crop like cotton one year, and then planting a soil restoring plant like peanuts, the next year.
    b. growing only one crop on the land year after year.
    c. nursing sick plants back to health
    d. studying plants at an institute.
    e. planting a large garden

Read the work instruction below, then answer questions 12-16.

JOB HAZARDS ANALYSIS

1.0 PURPOSE AND SCOPE

This procedure describes the Job Hazard Analysis (JHA) process for identifying, evaluating, controlling, and communicating potential hazards and environmental impacts associated with operations or work by the Tank Operations Contractor (TOC). It applies to all TOC work activities, including the performance of field work involving general plant maintenance, operations, and environmental remediation. This procedure applies to subcontractors who do not have an approved job hazard analysis process. Everyone is required to work safely and to maintain a safe work environment. Training procedures have been reviewed to ensure that workers are trained to the general hazards associated with work at the tank farms. Visitors should be briefed on the general safety hazards they may be exposed to and controls expected of them as part of their orientation.

2.0 IMPLEMENTATION

This procedure is effective on the date shown in the header.

3.0 RESPONSIBILITIES

Responsibilities are contained within Section 4.0.

4.0 Methods for Implementation of Controls

In order to effectively implement necessary controls to mitigate or eliminate hazards to the workers, the following guidelines should be used:

4.1. The following hierarchy of methods to eliminate or mitigate hazards shall be used in descending order, when feasible and appropriate:

1. Eliminate the hazard or substitution (e.g., different chemical cleaning agent)
2. Utilize engineering controls (e.g., ventilation)
3. Administrative controls (e.g., dose monitoring)
4. Personal protective equipment (PPE) (e.g., self-contained breathing apparatus)

4.2. Controls within the qualification or training of the worker that are often used do not need to be discussed in the work instructions. Examples: Use of leather gloves, safety glasses of the proper type that the worker normally uses.

4.3. Controls within the qualification or training of the worker that are seldom used, and are applicable to the entire work activity, should be placed in the precautions as a reminder that the hazard exists and the workers are expected to take the appropriate actions. Examples: Use of hearing protection due to a noisy environment at the job site, or observation of overhead lines when they are present at the job site.

4.4. Controls within the qualification and training of the workers, but for hazards that are introduced at specific steps or by specific actions during the job, should have a warning or caution statement immediately prior to the step but require no detailed mitigation instructions in the work instructions. Example: a warning for the release of pressure when breaching a system that may have residual pressure.

4.5. Controls not within the qualification and training of the workers for hazards should have detailed instructions for how the workers are to mitigate the hazard and should be in the work instructions or procedure in a way that is prominent and prevents or mitigates the hazard. Example: the steps required to successfully release the pressure on a system in an operation which is not normally performed.

12. This document is
   a. a government request for proposals
   b. a process for making rules for working safely
   c. a portion of a contract
   d. a set of rules for working efficiently

13. According to the procedure, if a worker is exposed to a hazardous chemical, which of the following is the last thing that should be tried to prevent injury or illness?

a. Use a different chemical.
b. Install fans to keep fumes away from the worker.
c. Measure the amount of exposure of each affected worker.
d. Give the worker protective clothing.

14. Welders must always use goggles and are taught to use them as part of their basic training. According to the text, the use of goggles during specific welding operations should

a. be prominently displayed at the beginning of the work instruction.
b. be displayed as a caution prior to the welding step described in the work instruction.
c. be described in detail in the work instruction.
d. not be discussed in the work instruction.

15. This passage would normally need to be read and understood by

a. managers at the site.
b. laborers at the site.
c. visitors to the site.
d. workers making deliveries to the site.

16. Which of the following requires the most comprehensive description within the work instructions?

a. Controls that are part of the worker's training and are used routinely
b. Controls that are part of the worker's training but that are seldom used
c. Controls that are part of the worker's training and that are required for specific steps in the work procedure
d. Controls that are not part of the worker's training

Read the following dialogue, then answer Questions 17-21.

DOCTOR

The Doctor and his wife come onstage quarreling.

Doctor: No, I tell you, I will do nothing of the kind. After all, I am the master.

Martine: And I tell you that I didn't go and marry you to put up with all your freaks.

Doctor: Oh, what an awful trouble it is to have a wife! How right Aristotle was when he said that a woman is worse than the devil!

Martine: Just listen to the clever man, with his fool of an Aristotle.

Doctor: Clever, indeed! You go and find a ditch-digger who can reason like me about everything, who has served for six years a most famous doctor, and who in his youth could say the Latin grammar by heart.

Martine: Plague take the fool!

Doctor: Plague take the wench!

Martine: Cursed be the day when I took it into my head to go and say "Yes!"

Doctor: Cursed be the old idiot who made me sign my ruin!

Martine: It becomes you well to complain of our marriage! You should thank Heaven every moment of your life for having me as a wife. And did you deserve, tell me, to marry a woman like me?

Doctor: True, indeed! You honored me too much, and I had reason to be satisfied on our wedding-day. Gad! Don't make me speak of it, or I might say certain things.

Martine: Well! What is it you'd say?

Doctor: Enough of that. It is sufficient that I know what I know, and that you were very lucky to have me.

Martine: What do you mean by my being lucky to have you? A man who reduces me to beggary; a debauched, deceitful villain, who eats up all I possess.

Doctor: That's a lie; I drink part of it.

Martine: Who sells, bit by bit, all that we have in the house.

Doctor: That is what is called living on one's means.

Martine: Who even sold the bed from under me.

Doctor: You'll get up all the earlier.

Martine: A man who does not leave a single stick of furniture in the house.

Doctor: We move about more easily.

Martine: And who does nothing from morning to night but drink and gamble.

Doctor: That's for fear of depression.

Martine: And what can I do with the children all the time?

Doctor: Anything you like.

Martine: I have four little ones on my hands.

Doctor: Put them down on the ground.

Martine: They do nothing but ask for bread.

Doctor: Whip them. When I have eaten and drunk my fill, I wish everybody to live on the fat of the land.

Martine (threatening, moves toward him): And do you think, drunkard, that things can always go on like this?

Doctor: Now, my wife, gently, if you please.

Martine: That I must endure forever your insolence and excesses.

Doctor (backing away): Do not get in a passion, my dear wife.

Martine: And that I shall not find the means of bringing you to a sense of your duty?

Doctor (standing his ground): My dear wife, you know that I am not very patient, and that I have a good strong arm.

17. This play is an example of a
   a. tragedy
   b. comedy
   c. drama
   d. soliloquy

18. When the Doctor curses "the old idiot who made me sign my ruin", he is referring to
   a. someone who loaned him money
   b. someone who sold him his house
   c. the clergyman who married him to Martine
   d. a government official

19. When Martine criticizes the Doctor's bad habits, such as drinking and gambling, his answers may be described as
   a. glib
   b. regretful
   c. defensive
   d. apologetic

20. Which of the following best describes the Doctor's personality?
   a. irascible
   b. intolerant
   c. irresponsible
   d. choleric

21. When Martine grows angry and moves toward him, threateningly, what is the Doctor's first response?
   a. He grows angry as well.
   b. He shows fear.
   c. He ignores her.
   d. He attempts to placate her.

Read the following passage, then answer questions 22-31:

In ancient times, the people hunted the buffalo on the Great Plains. These huge animals were their source of food and clothing. With stone-tipped spears, they stalked the great beasts through the tall grasses. It was difficult and dangerous work, but they were forced to do it in order to survive.

At that time, there were many crows flying above the plains, as there are today. But unlike the crows we see now, these birds were white. And they were friends to the buffalo, which caused the hunters no end of travail. The white crows flew high above the plains, where they could see all that was happening below. And when they saw that hunters were approaching the herd, they would warn the buffalo. Swooping down low, they would land on the heads of the great beasts and call out to them: "Beware! Beware! Hunters are coming from the south! Caw, caw. Beware!" And the buffalo would stampede, leaving the hunters empty-handed.

This went on for some time, until the people were hungry, and something needed to be done. A council was convened, and the chief of the people spoke to them. "We must capture the chief of the crows, and teach him a lesson, he said. If we can frighten him, he will stop warning the buffalo when our hunters approach, and the other crows will stop as well."

The old chief then brought out a buffalo skin, one with the head and horns still attached. "With this, we can capture the chief of the crows," he said. And he gave the skin to one of the tribe's young braves, a man known as Long Arrow. "Disguise yourself with this, and hide among the buffalo in the herd," the chief told Long Arrow. "Then, when the chief of the crows approaches, you will capture him and bring him back to the tribe."

So Long Arrow donned the buffalo skin disguise and went out onto the plains. Carefully, he approached a large herd of buffalo and mingled among them, pretending to graze upon the grasses. He moved slowly with the herd as they sought fresh food, and he waited for the great white bird that was the chief of the crows.

The other braves made ready for the hunt. They prepared their stone-tipped spears and arrows, and they approached the grazing herd of beasts, hiding in ravines and behind rocks to try to sneak up on them. But the crows, flying high in the sky, saw everything. The chief of the crows saw the men in the ravines and tall grasses, and eventually he came gliding down to warn the buffalo of the approaching hunters.

Hearing the great white crow's warning, the herd ran from the hunters. All stampeded across the plains except Long Arrow, still in his disguise. Seeing that Long Arrow remained, and thinking that he was a buffalo like all the others, the great white crow flew to him and landed upon his head. "Caw, caw. Hunters are approaching! Have you not heard my warning? Why do you remain here?" But as the great bird cried out, Long Arrow reached from under his disguise and grabbed the bird's feet, capturing him. He pushed him into a rawhide bag and brought him back to the tribal council.

The people debated what to do with the chief of the crows. Some wanted to cut his wings, so that he could not fly. Some wanted to kill him, and some wanted to remove his feathers as punishment for making the tribe go hungry. Finally, one brave strode forward in anger, grabbed the rawhide bag that held the bird, and before anyone could prevent it, threw it into the fire.

As the fire burned the rawhide bag, the big bird struggled to escape. Finally, he succeeded in getting out of the bag and managed to fly out of the fire, but his feathers were singed and covered with black soot from the fire. The chief of the crows was no longer white; he was black – as crows are today.

And from that day forward, all crows have been black. And although they fly above the plains and can see all that transpires below, they no longer warn the buffalo that hunters are approaching.

22. According to the passage, the people used stone spears to hunt the buffalo because
 a. They had no metal.
 b. They had no horses.
 c. They needed to eat.
 d. They were plentiful.

23. The word *travail* (Line 7) means
 a. Travel.
 b. Difficulty.
 c. Anger.
 d. Fear.

24. Which statement best describes what the chief of the crows represents in this passage?
 a. He symbolizes all that is evil.
 b. He is a symbol representing all crows.
 c. He represents the animal kingdom.
 d. He represents other predators who compete with the tribe.

25. Which of the following best describes the people's motivation for wanting to capture the chief of the crows?
 a. They hated birds.
 b. They wanted to turn him black.
 c. They wanted to eat him.
 d. They were hungry.

26. Long Arrow's activities among the herd while disguised imply that he
 a. Had time to kill.
 b. Wanted to fool the buffalo.
 c. Wanted to fool the crows.
 d. Had forgotten his stone-tipped spear.

27. In this tale, the rawhide bag and stone-tipped spears are both details that
 a. Are important for the outcome of the tale.
 b. Paint a picture of the primitive culture of the people.
 c. Make it clear that the people were dependent upon the buffalo.
 d. Show how the people hunted.

28. Why might the chief of the crows have landed upon Long Arrow's head after seeing the other buffalo stampede away?
 a. He thought his warning had not been heard.
 b. He wanted to see the disguise.
 c. He thought that Long Arrow was an injured buffalo.
 d. He had no fear of men.

29. Once the bird has been caught, what emotions are revealed by the people's deliberations about how to deal with him?

a. Anger
b. A calm resolve to change the birds' behavior
c. A feeling of celebration now that the bird has been caught
d. Hunger

30. What does the story tell us about why Long Arrow was selected for this task?

a. He was the bravest man in the tribe.
b. He was related to the chief.
c. He was able to act like a buffalo.
d. The story says nothing about why he was selected.

31. What does this story suggest that the American Indians thought of crows?

a. They were dirty animals.
b. They were clever animals.
c. They were selfish animals.
d. They disliked the people in the tribe.

Questions 32-38 are based on the following passage:

Zakov arrived at the prison shortly before noon, having dropped Ludmilla off at the train station beforehand. He was relieved to find that Gorkhi had gone, for he found the chief to be a bit bombastic, and was disposed to conduct the interrogation without him if he could. He was fortunate in that one of Gorkhi's men recognized him and let him in to see the prisoner.

He found the student sitting on the floor of a damp cell. The only illumination came from a small window set high in the concrete wall. Nasadev raised red-rimmed eyes when the door opened, amid a clatter of keys and bolts, and Zakov found himself again amazed at the lad's homeliness, rendered even more pathetic by features wet and swollen from weeping. Somewhat discomfited by his own reaction, he forced a smile.

The young man attempted to rise, but was hindered by the shackles about his ankles.

"Please, remain seated," offered Zakov quickly, and joined him on the earthen floor. "Ludmilla delivered your note. Just what kind of trouble are you in?"

"They are saying that I killed Olga," the youth replied, his face contorted in a grimace. "As if I could! I adored her," he cried. "But things look rather bleak for me, the way they found my knife. Only you can help me, sir. I know your reputation. Please help me, sir! Not for myself, but for my family. This will destroy them…" His tears welled up again, and he sniffled and dabbed vainly at his cheeks with his dirty sleeve.

Zakov looked at him sympathetically. Ludmilla had told him the student was pathetic, and she was right: the ordinary face, the weak chin, now damp with tears and perspiration, made him seem a most unlikely suitor. He must have been deeply hurt by Olga's rejection. And she, delicate, spirited and appealing, must have found his attentions tedious and annoying, the more so since he had neither fortune nor prospects. Had she derided him, mocked him, gone too far setting trial to his devotion until he killed her?

"What made the police suspect you?" he asked.

"They talked to some of the other students, and my name came up." Nasadev was almost whining. "One of them found a letter I had written, but never sent. He told the others. It made me angry, but I guess it was foolish of me to think that such a girl could ever like someone like me. But she was nice to me, nonetheless. She told me about the play she was writing, and how she hoped to go to Moscow."

Zakov found that his heart went out to the poor, infatuated youth. But pity was not enough to resolve the charges the student faced.

"So the other students mentioned your name," he continued. "That explains why the police spoke to you, but it's not enough for them to bring charges. What else happened?"

Nasadev replied plaintively, fixing Zakov with an imploring look. "We had a quarrel. In the park. The day before they found her. Someone must have heard us and they told the police. They came and searched my room in the dormitory, found my diary, some other letters I had written."

"What was the quarrel about?"

Nasadev hesitated, would not meet Zakov's eye. "I had asked her to marry me. I know it was crazy...how could I support her? But I was afraid she would stop seeing me, that someone else would come along and I would lose her."

"And what did she say?" Zakov knew the answer already, but he had to ask.

"She turned me down. She didn't laugh at me, but she turned me down. And that was in my diary, too." Nasadev was practically inaudible.

Zakov stayed a while longer, asked a few more questions. A deep sadness seemed to fill his heart as he regarded the small cell and its single miserable occupant. Finally, with a shiver, he called for Gorkhi's man to open the door and he left.

32. Zakov thought that Gorkhi, the police chief, was
a. considerate
b. pretentious
c. enthusiastic
d. moderate
e. uncooperative

33. **The passage suggests that Nasadev's cell**

   a. was modern
   b. had only a bed in it
   c. was spacious
   d. was unfurnished
   e. smelled badly

34. **Nasadev's frame of mind during the interview can best be described as**

   a. resigned
   b. courageous
   c. determined
   d. desperate
   e. calculating

35. **Zakov's attitude toward Nasadev appears to be one of**

   a. disgust
   b. magnanimity
   c. sympathy
   d. malice
   e. anger

36. **Nasadev's look, when he replies to Zakov's question (Line 40) implies that he is**

   a. begging for help
   b. about to collapse
   c. looking for words
   d. exhausted
   e. unable to think clearly

37. **When the student tells Zakov that Olga's rejection of his proposal was in the diary found by the police (Line 42), his voice**

   a. whines
   b. is hard to hear
   c. contains a signal
   d. breaks
   e. is a whisper

38. **By the time Zakov leaves, he**

   a. has proved Nasadev's guilt
   b. is angry at Gorkhi
   c. has found a possible motive for Nasadev to have committed the murder
   d. has proved Nasadev's innocence
   e. is late for a meeting with Ludmilla

Questions 39-40 are based on the following passage:

   Physically, at least, Hal seemed a most unlikely burglar. He looked more suited to the life of a professional athlete, the practitioner of some brutal contact sport. His legs were the trunks of ancient trees and his white shirts – he always wore white shirts – spread across is belly like the winter snow on an Alberta meadow. And yet, at night, he moved across the glistening rooftops on cat's feet, a passing shadow, dropping unseen to the topmost landing of fire escape or outside stairway. There, by starlight, his soft hands found whatever open window had been left unguarded and, in a matter of seconds, he would disappear inside.

39. The reference to tree trunks shows that

    a. Hal's legs were brown
    b. Hal's legs were made of wood
    c. Hal's wore pants the color of bark
    d. Hal's legs were very large
    e. Hal's skin was wrinkled

40. The passage describes Hal as moving on cat's feet. This means that

    a. he had fur-lined shoes
    b. he moved very quietly
    c. he stepped on a cat
    d. he was disguised
    e. he moved on all fours

Language Arts - Writing

Questions 1-6 are based on the following passage:

1) Family caregivers are the more than 65 million people in the United States that take care of other adults, often parents or spouses, or children with special medical needs. 2) Being a caregiver has high cost, however there are support services available.

3) Determine what stage of caregiving your family currently faces. 4) Than, before beginning the journey, a careful assessment of your loved one's condition will help you prepare for the challenges you will soon face. 5) The AARP (American Association of Retired Persons) provides a helpful checklist to ensure you get the entire picture.

6) The Family Care Navigator from the National Center on Caregiving will help you navigate the tedious spider's web of long-term care programs in your state. 7) As with most things in this day and age there are myriad options for how to care for your loved one. 8) Will you provide care in your home or their home, will you hire a professional or a family member, will the situation be temporary or permanent? 9) The scenarios are endless.

10) As primary care provider you'll help your loved one decide where to live. 11) Will they stay at home, or live with somewhere else? 12) Wherever they stay, make sure you do a home safety check. 13) Also, create an emergency plan, give all family members a copy, and make sure they know how to execute the plan should the need arise.

1. What is the best way to write the italicized part of sentence 1?

Family caregivers are the more than 65 million people in the United States *that take care of other adults, often parents or spouses, or children with special medical needs*.

   a. (As it is now)
   b. who take care of other adults, often parents or spouses or children with special medical needs.
   c. who take care of other adults, often parents or spouses, or children with special medical needs.
   d. which take care of other adults, often parents or spouses, or children with special medical needs.
   e. whom take care of other adults, often parents or spouses, or children with special medical needs.

2. Which is the best version of sentence 2?

Being a caregiver has high cost, however there are support services available.

   a. (As it is now)
   b. Being a caregiver has high cost, however there are supports services available.
   c. Being a caregiver has a high cost, however, there are support service available
   d. Being a caregiver has high cost however there are support services available.
   e. Being a caregiver has a high cost; however, there are support services available.

3. What is the best way to write the italicized part of sentence 4?

Than, before beginning the journey, a careful assessment of your loved one's condition will help you prepare for the challenges you will soon face.

   a. (As it is now)
   b. Than, before beginning the journey; a careful assessment of your loved one's condition will
   c. Then, before beginning the journey, a careful assessment of your loved one's condition will
   d. Then, before beginning the journey, a careful assessment of your loved ones condition will
   e. Then, before beginning the journey, a careful assessment of your loved one's condition have

4. Which is the best version of sentence 7?

As with most things in this day and age there are myriad options for how to care for your loved one.

   a. (As it is now)
   b. As with most things in these days and ages there are myriad options for how to care for your loved one.
   c. As with most things in this day and age, there are myriad options for how to care for your loved one.
   d. As with most things in this day and age there are myriad options from how to caring for your loved one.
   e. As with most things in this day and age, there is myriad options for how to care for your loved one.

5. Which is the best way to combine sentences 10 and 11?

As primary care provider you'll help your loved one decide where to live. Will they stay at home, or live with somewhere else?

   a. As primary care provider you'll help your loved one decide where to live and decide if they will stay at home or live somewhere else.
   b. As primary care provider; you'll help your loved one decide where to live and if they stay at home or live somewhere else.
   c. As primary care provider, you will help your loved one decide whether to stay at home or live somewhere else.
   d. Will they stay at home or live somewhere else; you will help your loved one decide.
   e. Will they stay at home or live somewhere else; you will help your loved one with the big decision.

6. What is the best way to write the italicized part of sentence 13?

Also, create an emergency plan, give all family members a copy, and make sure they know how to execute the plan should the need arise.

   a. (As it is now)
   b. and make sure they know when to execute the plan should the need arise.
   c. and make sure they know where to execute the plan should the need arise.
   d. and make sure they knew how to execute the plan should the need arise.
   e. and make sure to know how to execute the plan should the need arise.

Questions 7-12 are based on the following passage:

> 1) Just like having a working smoke detector in your home, have emergency supply kits will put the tools you may need at your fingertips. 2) Be prepared to improvise and use what you have on hand to make it on your own for at least three days,

maybe longer. 3) While there are many things that might make you more comfortable, think first about fresh water, food and clean air. 4) Remember to include, and periodically rotate medications you take every day such as insulin and heart medicine. 5) Plan to store items in an easy-to-carry bag, such as a shopping bag, backpack or duffle bag. 6) Store one gallon of water in clean plastic containers per person per day for drinking and sanitation. 7) If you live in a Warm Weather Climate more water may be necessary.

8) Store food that won't go bad and does not have to be heated or cooked. 9) Choose foods that your family will eat, including protein or fruit bars, dry cereal or granola, canned foods and juices, peanut butter, dried fruit, nuts, crackers and baby foods. 10) Remember to pack a manual can opener, cups and eating utensils.

11) Store a flashlight, battery powered radio, extra batteries, a first aid kit, utility knife, local map, toilet paper, feminine hygiene products, soap, garbage bags and other sanitation supplies, duct tape, as well as extra cash and identification. 12) Periodically rotate your extra batteries to be sure they work when you need them.

7. In context, which is the best version of sentence 1?

Just like having a working smoke detector in your home, have emergency supply kits will put the tools you may need at your fingertips.

   a. (As it is now)
   b. Just like having a working smoke detectors in your home, having emergency supply kits will put the tools you may need at your fingertips.
   c. Just like having a working smoke detector in your home, having emergency supply kits will put the tools you may need at your fingertips.
   d. Just like having a working smoke detector in your home, having emergency supply kit will put the tools you may need at your fingertips.
   e. Just like having a working smoke detector in your home; having emergency supply kits will put the tools you may need at your fingertips.

8. Which is the best way to write the italicized part of sentence 2?

Be prepared to improvise and use *what you have on hand to make it on your own for at least three days, maybe longer.*

   a. (As it is now)
   b. what you have on hand to make it on your own for at least three days; maybe longer.
   c. which you have on hand to make it on your own for at least three days, maybe longer.
   d. what you have on hand to make it on your own for at least three days', maybe longer.
   e. what you've have on hand to make it on your own for at least three days, maybe longer.

9. Which is the best version of sentence 4?

Remember to include, and periodically rotate medications you take every day such as insulin and heart medicine.

   a. (As it is now)
   b. Remember to include, and periodically rotate, medications you take every day such as insulin and heart medicine.
   c. Remember, to include and periodically rotate, medications you take every day such as insulin and heart medicine.
   d. Remember to include and periodically rotate medications you take every day such as insulin and heart medicine.
   e. Remember to include, and periodically rotate, medications you take every day such as insulin, and heart medicine.

10. In context, which is the best version of sentence 6?

Store one gallon of water in clean plastic containers per person per day for drinking and sanitation.

   a. (As it is now)
   b. Store one gallon of water in clean plastic containers for drinking and sanitation per person per day.
   c. Store one gallon of water per person per day in clean plastic containers for drinking and sanitation.
   d. For drinking and sanitation store one gallon of water per person per day, in clean plastic containers.
   e. Per person per day, store one gallon of water in clean plastic containers for drinking and sanitation.

11. Which is the best version of sentence 7?

If you live in a Warm Weather Climate more water may be necessary.

   a. (As it is now)
   b. If you live in a warmer weather climate more water may be necessary.
   c. If you live in a warm weather climate more water may be necessary.
   d. If you live in a warm weather Climate more water may be necessary.
   e. If you live in a warm weather climate, more water may be necessary.

12. Which sentence would be a good sentence to follow sentence 12?

Periodically rotate your extra batteries to be sure they work when you need them.

   a. Diapers, formula bottles, prescription medicine and pet food.
   b. If you live in a cold climate, we must think about warmth.
   c. Remember to feed the dog dry dog food every morning.
   d. If you live in a cold climate, have warm clothing on hand.
   e. Store one gallon of water per person per day for drinking.

Questions 13-18 are based on the following passage:

   1) Antibiotic drugs can save lives. 2) But some germs' get so strong that they can resist the drugs. 3) This is called resistance. 4) The drugs don't work even well. 5) Germs can even pass on resistance to other germs.

6) Antibiotic normally work by killing germs called bacteria, or stopping the bacteria from growing. 7) But sometimes not all of them are stopped or killed, and the strongest ones are left to grow and spread. 8) A person can get sick again, by which point the germs have become harder to kill.

9) The more often a person uses an antibiotic, more likely it is that the germs will resist it. 10) This can make some diseases very hard to control. 11) It can make people sick for longer periods and require more doctor visits and stronger drugs to treat the problem.

12) Bacteria and viruses are the two main types of germs. 13) They cause most illness. 14) Antibiotics can kill bacteria, but they do not work against viruses. 15) Viruses cause colds, coughs, sore throats, flu, bronchitis, ear infections and sinus problems. 16) If you have a virus, taking antibiotics is not recommended. 17) The medicine will not help you, in fact, it might even harm you. 18) Each time you take one, you add to the chances that bacteria in your body will be able to resist the antibiotic.

13. What is the best way to combine sentences 1, 2 and 3?
Antibiotic drugs can save lives. But some germs' get so strong that they can resist the drugs. This is called resistance.

  a. Antibiotic drugs, can save lives, but some germs' get so strong that they can resist the drugs and this is call resistance.
  b. Antibiotic drugs can save lives, but some germs' get so strong that they can resist the drugs, this is called resistance.
  c. Antibiotic drugs can save lives, but some germs get so strong that they can resist the drugs, which is called resistance.
  d. Antibiotic drugs can save lives but some germs get so strong that they can resists the drugs, which is called resistance.
  e. Antibiotic drugs can saves lives, but some germs get so strong than they can resist the drugs; this is called resistance.

14. Which is the best version of sentence 4?
The drugs don't work even well.

  a. (As it is now)
  b. The drugs don't work as well.
  c. The drugs don't work as better.
  d. The drugs don't work so good.
  e. The drugs don't not work as well.

15. Which is the best way to write the italicized part of sentence 6?
Antibiotic normally work by killing germs called bacteria, or stopping the bacteria from growing.

  a. (As it is now)
  b. Antibiotics normally work with killing germs called bacteria,
  c. Antibiotics normally work by killing germs called bacterias,
  d. Antibiotic's normally work by killing germs called bacteria,
  e. Antibiotics normally work by killing germs called bacteria,

16. Which is the best version of sentence 9?
The more often a person uses an antibiotic, more likely it is that the germs will resist it.

   a. (As it is now)
   b. The more often a person uses an antibiotic. The more likely it is that the germs will resist it.
   c. The more often a person uses an antibiotic, the more likelier it is that the germs will resist it.
   d. The more oftener a person uses an antibiotic, the more likely it is that the germs will resist it.
   e. The more often a person uses an antibiotic, the more likely it is that the germs will resist it.

17. Which is the best version of sentence 17?
The medicine will not help you, in fact, it might even harm you.

   a. (As it is now)
   b. The medicine will not help you. In fact, it might even harm you.
   c. The medicine will not help you in fact. It might even harm you.
   d. The medicine will not help you in fact it might even harm you.
   e. The medicine willn't help you. In fact, it might even harm you.

18. Which sentence would best follow sentence 18?
Each time you take one, you add to the chances that bacteria in your body will be able to resist the antibiotic.

   a. Lyme disease, tuberculosis (TB) and bacterial pneumonia.
   b. Doctors are always very busy and in a hurry.
   c. Later, that could make you very sick.
   d. Don't take someone else's medicine.
   e. FDA stands for the Food and Drug Administration.

Questions 19-24 are based on the following passage:

   1) Most adults needing at least eight hours of sleep every night to be well rested. 2) Not everyone gets the sleep they need. 3) About 40 million people in the United States suffer from sleep problems every year. 4) Not getting enough sleep for an extended period of time can cause health problems. 5) It can make problems like diabetes and high blood pressure worse. 6) Many things can disturb your sleep. 7) Stress, a sick child, working long hours, or light or noise from traffic or TV.

   8) One type of sleep problem is called insomnia. 9) Insomnia symptoms include trouble falling asleep, having trouble getting back to sleep and waking up too early.

   10) Most people have trouble falling asleep from time to time. 11) Stress, like the loss of a job or a death in the family, could cause problems falling asleep. 12) Certain medicines can also make it hard to fall asleep. 13) Drinking alcohol or eating too close to bedtime can keep you awake, too. 14) Insomnia is called chronic, or long-term, when it lasts most nights for a few weeks or more. 15) You should see your doctor if this happens. 16) Insomnia is more common in Females, people with Depression, and in people older than 60. 17) Taking medicine together with making changes to a routine can help most people with insomnia.

19. In context, which is the best version of sentence 1?

Most adults needing at least eight hours of sleep every night to be well rested.

a. (As it is now)
b. Most adults need at least eight hours of sleep every night being well rested.
c. Most adults needing at least eight hours of sleep every night been well rested.
d. Most adults need at least eight hours of sleep every night to be well rested.
e. Most adults to need at least eight hours of sleep every night to be well rested.

20. Which is best added to the beginning of sentence 5?

It can make problems like diabetes and high blood pressure worse.

a. Possibly
b. Hardly ever
c. Nevertheless
d. As a result
e. For example

21. Which is the best version of sentences 6 and 7?

Many things can disturb your sleep. Stress, a sick child, working long hours, or light or noise from traffic or TV.

a. (As it is now)
b. Many things can disturb your sleep, stress, a sick child, and working long hours. Or light or noise from traffic or TV.
c. Many things can disturb your sleep; stress, a sick child, working long hours, or light or noise from traffic or TV.
d. Many things can disturb your sleep and stress, a sick child working long hours, or light or noise from traffic or TV.
e. Many things can disturb your sleep, such as stress, a sick child, working long hours, or light or noise from traffic or TV.

22. In context, which is the best version of sentence 11?

Stress, like the loss of a job or a death in the family, could cause problems falling asleep.

a. (As it is now)
b. Stress, liking the loss of a job or a death in the family, could cause problems falling asleep.
c. Stress, concerning the loss of a job or a death in the family, could cause problems falling asleep.
d. Stress, until the loss of a job or a death in the family, could cause problems falling asleep.
e. Stress, likely the loss of a job or a death in the family, could cause problems falling asleep.

23. Which is the best version of sentence 16?

Insomnia is more common in Females, people with Depression, and in people older than 60.

a. (As it is now)
b. Insomnia is more common in Females, people with depression, and in people older than 60.
c. Insomnia is more common in females, people with depression, and in people older than 60.
d. Insomnia is more common in females, people with Depression, and in people older than 60.
e. Insomnia is more common in females, people with depression, but in people older than 60.

24. Which would be the best sentence to follow sentence 17?

Taking medicine together with making changes to a routine can help most people with insomnia.

a. Doctors will advise you to get as much sleep as you can every night.
b. Geography class sometimes makes me feel very sleepy.
c. There are certain drugs that work in the brain to help promote sleep.
d. Make sure you have finished your homework before going to bed.
e. A new class of drugs called non-benzodiazepine hypnotics.

Questions 25-30 are based on the following passage:

1) Fish and shellfish are an important part of an healthy diet. 2) They contain high quality protein and other essential nutrients, and may contain omega-3 fatty acids. 3) In fact, a well-balanced diet that included a variety of fish and shellfish can contribute to heart health and children's growth and development.

4) But, as with any type of food, its important to handle seafood safely in order to reduce the risk of foodborne illness. 5) Follow these basic food safety tips for buying, preparing, and storing fish and shellfish and you and your family can safely enjoy the fine taste and good nutrition of seafood.

6) Buying from a retailer that follows proper food handling practices helps assure that the seafood you buy is safe and helps maintain the quality of the seafood, too. 7) Be sure to look at a market's seafood counter carefully to see whether the seller is practicing proper food handling techniques. 8) Ask yourself: What is my general impression of this facility? 9) Does it look and smell clean?

10) To be sure the safety of seafood is being properly preserved, only buy fish that is refrigerated or properly iced. 11) Fish should be displayed on a thick bed of fresh ice that is not melting, and preferably in a case or under some type of cover.

12) Fish should smell fresh and mild, not fishy, sour, or ammonia-like. 13) Whole fish and fillets should have firm, shiny flesh and bright red gills free of slime. 14) Dull flesh could mean the fish is old.

25. Which is the best version of sentence 1?

Fish and shellfish are an important part of an healthy diet.

a. (As it is now)
b. Fish and shellfish are an important part of and healthy diet.
c. Fish and shellfish, are an important part of a healthy diet.
d. Fish and shellfish are an important part of a healthy diet.
e. Fish and shellfish are an important part of a healthy diets.

26. Which is the best version of the italicized part of sentence 3?

In fact, a well-balanced diet that included a variety of fish and shellfish can contribute to heart health and children's growth and development.

   a. (As it is now)
   b. In fact, a well-balance diet; they include a variety of fish and shellfish can contribute to
   c. In fact, a well-balanced diet than includes a variety of fish and shellfish can contribute to
   d. In fact, a well-balanced diet that includes a variety of fish and shellfish can contribute to
   e. In fact, a well-balanced diet which includes a variety of fish and shellfish can contribute to

27. Which is the best version of the italicized part of sentence 4?

But, as with any type of food, its important to handle seafood safely in order to reduce the risk of foodborne illness.

   a. (As it is now)
   b. But, as with any type of food, it's important handling seafood safely
   c. But, as with any type of food, it's importantly to handle seafood safely
   d. But, as with any type of food, it's important to handle seafood safe
   e. But, as with any type of food, it's important to handle seafood safely

28. Which is the best version of sentence 8?

Ask yourself: What is my general impression of this facility?

   a. (As it is now)
   b. Ask yourself: what is my general impression of this facility?
   c. Ask yourself? What is my general impression of this facility?
   d. Ask yourself what is my general impression of this facility?
   e. Ask yourself, what is my general impression of this facility?

29. In context, which is the best version of sentence 10?

To be sure the safety of seafood is being properly preserved, only buy fish that is refrigerated or properly iced.

   a. (As it is now)
   b. Being sure the safety of seafood is being properly preserved, only buy fish that is refrigerated or properly iced.
   c. To be sure the safety of seafood is being properly preserve, only buy fish that is refrigerated or properly iced.
   d. To be sure the safety of seafood is being properly preserving, only buy fish that is refrigerated or properly iced.
   e. To be sure the safety of seafood is being properly preserved, only buying fish that is refrigerated or properly iced.

30. Which of the following sentences best follows sentence 14?

Dull flesh could mean the fish is old.

   a. My mom makes the best fish fillets by broiling them in butter.
   b. If the catch has been left out in the hot sun for too much time.
   c. Health wise, it is important to look for freshness when choosing seafood.
   d. In the late afternoon, the fishermen turned around and returned to shore.
   e. There is a new seafood restaurant that is opening soon across the street.

Questions 31-36 are based on the following passage:

1) Every year in the United States, about 3,000 people lose their lives in residential fires. 2) In a fire, smoke and deadly gases tend to spread farther and faster than heat. 3) That's one reason why most fire victims die from inhalation of smoke and toxic gases instead of from burns. 4) A majority of fatal fires happen when families are asleep because occupants are unaware of the fire until their is not adequate time to escape. 5) A smoke alarm stands guard around the clock and sounds a shrill alarm as soon as it senses smoke. 6) This often allows a family the precious but limited time it takes to escape.

7) About two-thirds of home fire deaths occur in homes with no smoke alarms or no working smoke alarms. 8) Properly installed and maintained smoke alarms are considered to be one of the best and least expensive means of providing an early warning of a potentially deadly fire. 9) They can reduce the risk of dying from a fire in your home by almost half.

10) A smoke alarm is critical for the early detection of a fire in your home and could mean the difference between life and death. 11) Fires can occur for a variety of ways and in any room of your home.

31. In context, which is the best version of sentence 1?

Every year in the United States, about 3,000 people lose their lives in residential fires.

a. (As it is now)
b. Every year in the United States, in residential fires, about 3,000 people lose their lives.
c. About 3,000 people every year in the United States in residential fires lose their lives.
d. Every year in the United States lose their lives in residential fires about 3,000 people.
e. Every year in the United States: about 3,000 people lose their lives in residential fires.

32. Which is best added to the beginning of sentence 2?

In a fire, smoke and deadly gases tend to spread farther and faster than heat.

a. In fact
b. Although
c. Instead of
d. On the other hand
e. However

33. Which is the best version of the italicized part of sentence 4?

A majority of fatal fires happen when families are asleep because occupants are unaware of the fire until their is not adequate time to escape.

a. (As it is now)
b. because occupants are unaware of the fire until their are not adequate time to escape.
c. because occupants is unaware of the fire until their is not adequate time to escape.
d. because occupants are unaware of the fire, until there is not adequate, time to escape.
e. because occupants are unaware of the fire until there is not adequate time to escape.

34. Which is the best version of sentence 7?

About two-thirds of home fire deaths occur in homes with no smoke alarms or no working smoke alarms.

   a. (As it is now)
   b. About two-thirds of home fire deaths occurring in homes with no smoke alarms or no working smoke alarms.
   c. About two-thirds of home fire deaths occur; in homes with no smoke alarms or no working smoke alarms.
   d. About two-thirds of home fire deaths, occur in homes with no smoke alarms or no working smoke alarms.
   e. About two-thirds of home fire deaths occurs in homes with no smoke alarms or no working smoke alarms.

35. What is the best way to combine sentences 8 and 9?

Properly installed and maintained smoke alarms are considered to be one of the best and least expensive means of providing an early warning of a potentially deadly fire. They can reduce the risk of dying from a fire in your home by almost half.

   a. Properly installed and maintained smoke alarms are considered to be one of the best and least expensive means of providing an early warning of a potentially deadly fire although they can reduce the risk of dying from a fire in your home by almost half.
   b. Properly installed and maintained smoke alarms are considered to be one of the best and least expensive means of providing an early warning of a potentially deadly fire because they can reduce the risk of dying from a fire in your home by almost half.
   c. Properly installed and maintained smoke alarms are considered to be one of the best and least expensive means of providing an early warning of a potentially deadly fire rather than they can reduce the risk of dying from a fire in your home by almost half.
   d. Properly installed and maintained smoke alarms are considered to be one of the best and least expensive means of providing an early warning of a potentially deadly fire instead of reducing the risk of dying from a fire in your home by almost half.
   e. Properly installed and maintained smoke alarms are considered to be one of the best and least expensive means of providing an early warning of a potentially deadly fire as well as they can reduce the risk of dying from a fire in your home by almost half.

36. Which sentence best follows sentence 11?

Fires can occur for a variety of ways and in any room of your home.

   a. Most smoke alarms run on batteries but some are hardwired as well.
   b. Having a smoke alarm is the first key step towards your family's safety.
   c. Some fires occur as a result of poor or old-fashioned wiring.
   d. Many people like to use candles for atmosphere, but they can be dangerous.
   e. When people leave the house they should be sure that they turn off all the lights.

Questions 37-42 are based on the following passage:

   1) Searching for the perfect gifts online, instead of running from store to store, can save time, money and energy. 2) As with all purchases, though, it pays to comparison shop. 3) The Internet can make comparison shopping easy with sites like PriceGrabber.com, Amazon.com, Google Product Search, and PriceSpider.com, which allows you to see the price history of an item.

4) Even if you prefer to shop in brick and mortar stores, doing online research can help you save money a prepared shopper is one who gets more for his money. 5) And, with the advent of smart phones and shopping apps, comparison shopping goes to a whole new level because they allow you to comparison shop on the fly as you peruse the shelves and racks in your favorite store. 6) If that doesn't give the consumer power, what does?

7) Before making a final purchase decision, read through some online reviews. 8) When reading reviews, be conscious of the fact that companies sometimes compensating consumers to use their products and then provide reviews. 9) An unbiased review is best, but reading about many experiences will still help you get the whole picture.

10) Do you recognize the name of the online retailer or know its reputation? 11) Do you have friends or family members who have used the same company? 12) Read online reviews of the e-tailer if you have never ordered from them before. 13) Look for sellers who participate in programs that encourage good business practices, such as those sponsored by the Better Business Bureau.

37. In context, which is the best version of sentence 1?

Searching for the perfect gifts online, instead of running from store to store, can save time, money and energy.

a. (As it is now)
b. Instead of running from store to store, can save time, money and energy, searching for the perfect gifts online.
c. Can save time, money and energy, searching for the perfect gifts online instead of running from store to store.
d. Instead of running from store to store, searching for the perfect gifts, can save time, money and energy.
e. Instead of searching for the perfect gifts online, running from store to store can save time, money and energy.

38. Which is the best version of the italicized part of sentence 4?

Even if you prefer to shop in brick and mortar stores, doing online research can help you save money a prepared shopper is one who gets more for his money.

a. (As it is now)
b. brick and mortar stores, doing online research can help you save money, a prepared shopper is one who gets more for his money.
c. brick and mortar stores, doing online research can help you save money; a prepared shopper is one who gets more for his money.
d. brick and mortar; stores doing online research can help you save money a prepared shopper is one who gets more for his money.
e. brick and mortar stores, doing online research can help you save money although a prepared shopper is one who gets more for his money.

39. Which sentence would be best after sentence 7?

Before making a final purchase decision, read through some online reviews.

    a. Many people like to write reviews of restaurants where they have eaten.
    b. Information on real life product experience can be a helpful shopping tool.
    c. Reviews don't really tell you very much at all about products.
    d. Read at least two good reviews about each product.
    e. Shopping online can be tiresome.

40. Which is the best version of sentence 8?

When reading reviews, be conscious of the fact that companies sometimes compensating consumers to use their products and then provide reviews.

    a. (As it is now)
    b. When reading reviews, be conscious of the fact that companies sometimes is compensating consumers to use their products and then provide reviews.
    c. When reading reviews, be conscious of the fact that companies sometimes was compensating consumers to use their products and then provide reviews.
    d. When reading reviews, be conscious of the fact that companies sometimes compensate consumers to use their products and then provide reviews.
    e. When reading reviews, be conscious of the fact that companies sometimes compensates consumers to use their products and then provide reviews.

41. Which is the best version of sentence 12?

Read online reviews of the e-tailer if you have never ordered from them before.

    a. (As it is now)
    b. Read online reviews' of the e-tailer if you have never ordered from them before.
    c. Read online reviews of the e-tailer if you've never order from them before.
    d. Read online reviews of the e-tailer even if you've never ordered from them before.
    e. Read online reviews of the e-tailer if you have never order from them before.

42. Which is best added to the beginning of sentence 13?

Look for sellers who participate in programs that encourage good business practices, such as those sponsored by the Better Business Bureau.

    a. Consequently
    b. However
    c. Rarely
    d. Instead of
    e. Finally

Questions 43-48 are based on the following passage:

    1) Over the past two decades, restaurant portion sizes have significant increased. 2) And studies show that when individuals are served larger portions, they tend to eat more in a given sitting than when they are served smaller meals. 3) Unless you're careful, you can easily consume two or three times the amount of food at a restaurant than you might serve yourself at home. 4) The "value meal" only makes this problem worse. 5) Economically, spending only pennies more for a larger portion makes sense however, these portions can be a diet landmine.

6) There are ways to keep your portions in check. 7) For example, split an entrée with a family member or friend, and order a side salad or extra vegetables' to round out your meal. 8) You could also save half of your meal for later. 9) Just ask for a box at the beginning of the meal and immediately put away what you want to save if you doubt your ability to leave it on the plate. 10) Suggestions like these will keep you on the right track.

43. Which is the best version of sentence 1?

Over the past two decades, restaurant portion sizes have significant increased.

   a. (As it is now)
   b. Over the past two decades, restaurant portion sizes have significantly increased.
   c. Over the past two decades restaurant portion sizes have significantly increased.
   d. Over the past two decades, restaurant portion sizes have significant increases.
   e. Over the past two decades, restaurant portion sizes has significant increased.

44. In context, which is the best version of sentence 2?

And studies show that when individuals are served larger portions, they tend to eat more in a given sitting than when they are served smaller meals.

   a. (As it is now)
   b. And studies show when they are served smaller meals they tend to eat more in a given sitting than   when individuals are served larger portions.
   c. When they are served smaller meals, studies show, individuals are served larger portions and they tend to eat more in a given sitting.
   d. And studies show that when individuals are served larger portions, in a given sitting, they tend to eat more than when they are served smaller meals.
   e. When individuals, in a given sitting, are served larger portions, they tend to eat more than when they are served smaller meals and studies show that.

45. Which is best added to the beginning of sentence 4?

The "value meal" only makes this problem worse.

   a. Happily
   b. However
   c. Although
   d. In spite of
   e. Unfortunately

46. Which is the best version of the italicized part of sentence 5?

Economically, spending only pennies more *for a larger portion makes sense however, these portions can be a diet landmine.*

   a. (As it is now)
   b. for a larger portion makes sense, however, these portions can be a diet landmine.
   c. for a larger portion makes sense; however, these portions can be a diet landmine.
   d. for a larger portion make sense. However, these portions can be a diet landmine.
   e. for a larger portion makes sense however these portions can be a diet landmine.

47. Which is the best version of sentence 7?

For example, split an entrée with a family member or friend, and order a side salad or extra vegetables' to round out your meal.

- a. (As it is now)
- b. For example, split an entrée with a family member or friend; and order a side salad or extra vegetables to round out your meal.
- c. For example, split an entrée with a family member or friend, and ordering a side salad or extra vegetables' to round out your meal.
- d. For example, split an entrées with a family member or friend, and order a side salad or extra vegetables to round out your meal.
- e. For example, split an entrée with a family member or friend, and order a side salad or extra vegetables to round out your meal.

48. Which sentence best follows sentence 9?

Just ask for a box at the beginning of the meal and immediately put away what you want to save if you doubt your ability to leave it on the plate.

- a. The best restaurants will cook their food in the way you would like it.
- b. People continue to eat at fast food restaurants and eat more than they should.
- c. Some fast food restaurants use oil that is not good for your nutrition.
- d. Another trick is to order a kid's meal at a fast food restaurant and pay less to eat less.
- e. Food is a subject that never gets boring.

Questions 49-50 are based on the following passage:

1) The United States Department of Agriculture Forest Service has reached a milestone. 2) It now protects more than two million acres of private forests threatened by development. 3) *The Forest Service's Northeastern Area helped the agency reach the milestone* when the state of Ohio purchased a 15,494-acre property as the new Vinton Furnace State Experimental Forest approximately 90 miles south of Columbus. 4) The milestone was achieved through public-private partnership *using federal and leveraged funds of approximately $1.1 billion through the Forest legacy program.* 5) The Legacy program has leveraged the federal investment of more than 50 percent of project costs. 6) To date, through non-federal matching funds, to these efforts, more than $630 million has been contributed.

7) The Forest Legacy program works with private landowners, states and conservation groups to promote sustainable, working forests. 8) Roughly 57 percent of the nation's forests are privately owned, yet the country has lost 15 million acres of private working forests in the last 10 years, with an additional 22 million acres projected to be at risk in the next decade. 9) The Forest Legacy has protected millions of acres of privately owned forests that could have been turned into strip malls and housing developments, say Forest Service experts. 10) They say there have been many success stories, which they are proud of.

49. Which sentence best follows sentence 8?

Roughly 57 percent of the nation's forests are privately owned, yet the country has lost 15 million acres of private working forests in the last 10 years, with an additional 22 million acres projected to be at risk in the next decade.

    a. Some trees are harder to protect than others.
    b. Most successes were achieved through a public/private partnership.
    c. It's wonderful to see a forest of trees that is undisturbed.
    d. New machinery makes the creation of strip malls much easier.
    e. But not all is bad news about tree preservation at all.

50. What best goes at the beginning of sentence 10?

They say there have been many success stories, which they are proud of.

    a. For that reason
    b. Nevertheless
    c. For example
    d. However
    e. Although

Essay

A study conducted by a non-profit foundation examined teenagers' socializing on the Internet. The study found that most teenagers turn on their computers as soon as they return home from school every day, and that they use social media sites, as well as text messaging, to stay in touch with their circle of friends almost constantly throughout the day. Since many parents believe that internet socializing is a waste of time, the teenagers were subject to many restrictions, but they usually found ways to circumvent these rules.

In your essay, select either of these points of view, or suggest an alternative approach, and make a case for it. Use specific reasons and appropriate examples to support your position and to show how it is superior to the others.

Mathematics

1. What is the next-highest prime number after 67?

　a. 68
　b. 69
　c. 71
　d. 73
　e. 76

2. Dean's Department Store reduces the price of a $30 shirt by 20%, but later raises it again by 20% of the sale price. What is the final price of the shirt?

　a. $24.40
　b. $32
　c. $30
　d. $28.80
　e. $26.60

3. How many 3-inch segments can a 4.5-yard line be divided into?

　a. 15
　b. 45
　c. 54
　d. 64
　e. 84

4. Sheila, Janice, and Karen, working together at the same rate, can complete a job in 3 1/3 days. Working at the same rate, how much of the job could Janice and Karen do in one day?

　a. 1/5
　b. 1/4
　c. 1/3
　d. 1/9
　e. 1/8

5. Of the following expressions, which is equal to $6\sqrt{10}$?

　a. 36
　b. $\sqrt{600}$
　c. $\sqrt{360}$
　d. $\sqrt{6}$
　e. $10\sqrt{6}$

6. A box of laundry detergent contains 16.5 oz of product. What is the maximum number of loads that can be washed if each load requires a minimum of ¾ oz of detergent?

　a. 10
　b. 50
　c. 22
　d. 18
　e. 16.5

7. There are *n* musicians in a marching band. All play either a drum or a brass instrument. If *p* represents the fraction of musicians playing drums, how many play a brass instrument?
   a. $pn - 1$
   b. $p(n - 1)$
   c. $(p - 1)n$
   d. $(p + 1)n$
   e. $(1 - p)n$

8. Given the triangle shown in the figure, what is the length of the side *B*?

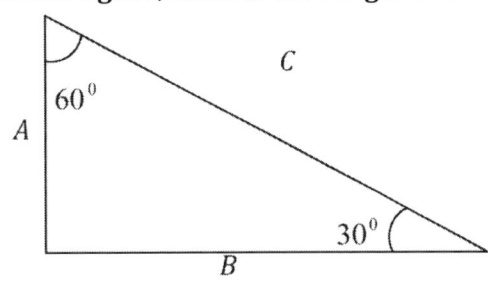

   a. $C/2$
   b. $A/2$
   c. $(A + C)/2$
   d. $2A$
   e. $2C$

9. A bullet travels at 5×10^6 feet per hour. If it strikes its target in 2×10^{-4} hours, how far has it traveled?
   a. 50 feet
   b. 25 feet
   c. 100 feet
   d. 1000 feet
   e. 200 feet

10. If 3a + 5b = 98 and a = 11, what is the value of a + b?

11. If the two lines $2x + y = 0$ and $y = 3$ are plotted on a typical *xy* coordinate grid, at which point will they intersect?
    a. -1.5, 3
    b. 1.5, 3
    c. -1.5, 0
    d. 4, 1
    e. 4.5, 1

12. Which of the following equations describes a line that is parallel to the *x*-axis?
    a. $y = 3$
    b. $y = 2x$
    c. $(x + y) = 0$
    d. $y = -3x$
    e. None of the above

109

13. How many identical cubes, each with edges of 3 inches, can fit in a box measuring 15 inches by 9 inches by 6 inches?

14. A blouse normally sells for $138, but is on sale for 25% off. What is the cost of the blouse?
   a. $67
   b. $103.50
   c. $34.50
   d. $113
   e. $125

15. $|7 - 5| - |5 - 7| =$
   a. 0
   b. 4
   c. 2
   d. -2
   e. -4

16.

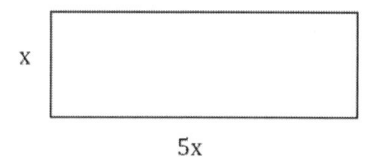

The above figure is a rectangle with an area of 245. What is the length of the longest side of the rectangle?

17. What is the average of $\frac{7}{5}$ and 1.4?
   a. 5.4
   b. 1.4
   c. 2.4
   d. 7.4
   e. None of these

18. What is the surface area, in square inches, of a cube if the length of one side is 3 inches?
   a. 9
   b. 27
   c. 54
   d. 18
   e. 21

19. If it took Lex from 10:00a.m. to 11:45a.m. to walk 14 blocks, what was his average speed in blocks per hour?

20. Which of the following values is closest to the diameter of a circle with an area of 314 square inches?
   a. 20 inches
   b. 10 inches
   c. 100 inches
   d. 31.4 inches
   e. 2π inches

21. The following table shows the distance from a point to a moving car at various times.

d	Distance	50	70	110
t	Time	2	3	5

If the speed of the car is constant, which of the following equations describes the distance from the point to the car?
   a. $d = 25 t$
   b. $d = 35 t$
   c. $d = 55 t$
   d. $d = 20 t + 10$
   e. None of these

22. The average of 4, 7, 9 and x is 9. What is the value of x?

23. A circle has a perimeter of 35 feet. What is its diameter?
   a. 11.14 feet
   b. 6.28 feet
   c. 5.57 feet
   d. 3.5 feet
   e. 14 feet.

24. A jar contains pennies and nickels. The ratio of nickels to pennies is 6:2. What percent of the coins are pennies?

25. What is the sum of the largest prime factor of 42 and the smallest prime factor of 42?

26. $4^6 \div 2^8 =$
   a. 2
   b. 8
   c. 16
   d. 32
   e. 64

27. If $a = 4$, $b = 3$, and $c = 1$, then $\frac{a(b-c)}{b(a+b+c)} =$
   a. 4/13
   b. 1/3
   c. 1/4
   d. 1/6
   e. 2/7

28. What is 20% of $\frac{12}{5}$, expressed as a percentage?

   a. 48%
   b. 65%
   c. 72%
   d. 76%
   e. 84%

29. Which number equals 2^{-3}?

   a. ½
   b. ¼
   c. 1/8
   d. 1/16
   e. 1/12

30. The flower shop puts all flowers in bouquets of 12. If the shop has 137 flowers, how many are left over when there aren't enough to make a full bouquet?

Questions 31-33 are based upon the following diagram of a circle, where O is the center and OA and OC are radii:

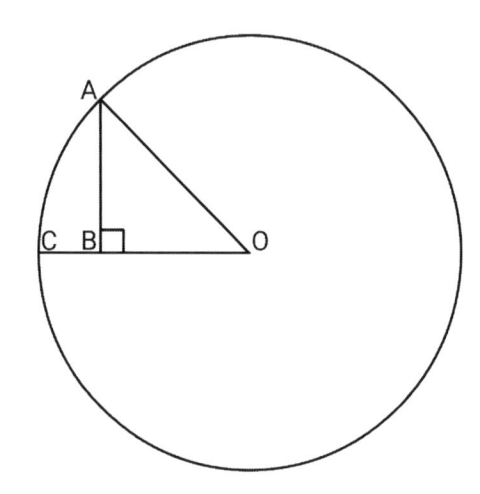

31. If the length of segment AB = x, and the length of segment OB = y, which of the following expressions describes the radius of the circle?

   a. $x + y$
   b. $x^2 + y^2$
   c. $y + 4 + 4$
   d. $\sqrt{x^2 + y^2}$
   e. $\sqrt{x^2 + 1}$

32. If the length of segment AB equals that of segment OB, what is the angle AOC?

   a. 45 degrees
   b. Same as angle BAO
   c. Same as angle ABO
   d. All the above are true
   e. A and B are true but not C

112

33. Which of the following must be true?
    a. OA = OC
    b. OB = BC
    c. OB = OC
    d. AB = OC
    e. None of the above

34. What fractional part of an hour is 400 seconds?
    a. 1/5
    b. 1/6
    c. 1/7
    d. 1/8
    e. 1/9

35. Larry gave 1/4 of his Halloween candy to his little sister Eva and 1/5 to his mom. What percentage of his Halloween candy did Larry have left?

36. A straight line with slope +4 is plotted on a standard Cartesian (*xy*) coordinate system so that it intersects the *y*-axis at a value of *y* = 1. Which of the following points will the line pass through?
    a. (2,9)
    b. (0,-1)
    c. (0,0)
    d. (4,1)
    e. (1,4)

37. A crane raises one end of a 3300 lb steel beam. The other end rests upon the ground. If the crane supports 30% of the beam's weight, how many pounds does it support?
    a. 330 lbs
    b. 990 lbs
    c. 700 lbs
    d. 1100 lbs
    e. 2310 lbs

38. Two angles of a triangle measure 15 and 70 degrees, respectively. What is the size of the third angle
    a. 90 degrees
    b. 80 degrees
    c. 75 degrees.
    d. 125 degrees
    e. 95 degrees

39. If 24 people tried to climb a mountain and 6 people completed the climb, what percentage of people didn't climb the mountain?

40. The triangle shown in the figure has angles A, B, and C, and sides *a*, *b*, and *c*. If *a* = 14 cm and *b* = 12 cm, and if angle ∠B = 35 degrees, what is angle ∠A?

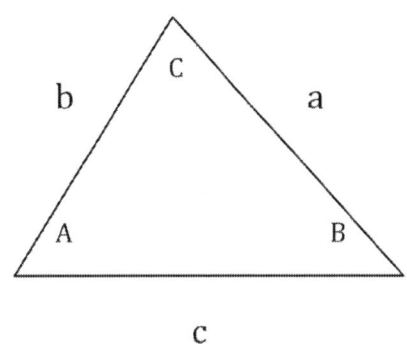

a. 35 degrees
b. 42 degrees
c. 64 degrees
d. 18 degrees
e. 28 degrees

41. A metal rod used in manufacturing must be as close a possible to 15 inches in length. The tolerance of the length, *L*, in inches, is specified by the inequality | *L* − 15 | ≤ 0.01. What is the minimum length permissible for the rod?

a. 14.9 inches
b. 14.99 inches
c. 15.01 inches
d. 15.1 inches
e. Inches

42. Two numbers are said to be reciprocal if their product equals 1. Which of the following represents the reciprocal of the variable *x* ?

a. $x - 1$
b. $\frac{1}{x}$
c. x^{-1}
d. x^{-2}
e. Both B and C.

43. A taxi service charges $5.50 for the first 1/5th of a mile, $1.50 for each additional 1/5th of a mile, and 20¢ per minute of waiting time. Joan took a cab from her place to a flower shop 8 miles away, where she bought a bouquet, then another 3.6 miles to her mother's place. The driver had to wait 9 minutes while she bought the bouquet. What was the fare?

a. $20
b. $120.20
c. $92.80
d. $91
e. $90

44. Which of the following expressions is equivalent to the equation $3x^2 + 4x - 15$?

 a. $(x - 3)(x + 5)$
 b. $(x + 5)(3 + x^2)$
 c. $x(3x^2 + 4 - 15)$
 d. $(3x^2 + 5)(x - 5)$
 e. $(x + 3)(3x - 5)$

45. It takes Roxana 1 hour and 30 minutes to ride her bike on the uphill trip to the park at an average speed of 4 miles per hour. If she comes home on the same route at an average speed of 5 miles per hour, how long in minutes does the return trip take?

 a. 52
 b. 62
 c. 72
 d. 82
 e. 92

46. An MP3 player is set to play songs at random from the fifteen songs it contains in memory. Any song can be played at any time, even if it is repeated. There are 5 songs by Band A, 3 songs by Band B, 2 by Band C, and 5 by Band D. If the player has just played two songs in a row by Band D, what is the probability that the next song will also be by Band D?

 a. 1 in 5
 b. 1 in 3
 c. 1 in 9
 d. 1 in 27
 e. Not enough data to determine.

47. Referring again to the MP3 player described in Question 46, what is the probability that the next two songs will both be by Band B?

 a. 1 in 25
 b. 1 in 3
 c. 1 in 5
 d. 1 in 9
 e. Not enough data to determine.

48. Which of the following expressions is equivalent to $3\left(\frac{6x-3}{3}\right) - 3(9x + 9)$?

 a. $-3(7x + 10)$
 b. $-3x + 6$
 c. $(x + 3)(x - 3)$
 d. $3x^2 - 9$
 e. $15x - 9$

49. A circle is inscribed within a square, as shown. What is the difference between the area of the square and that of the circle, where *r* is the radius of the circle?

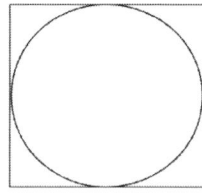

a. $2\pi\pi$
b. $\frac{4}{3}\pi r^3$
c. $r^2(4-\pi)$
d. $2\pi r$
e. $2r^2$

50. A two-digit number is chosen at random. What is the probability that the chosen number is a multiple of 7?

a. 1/10
b. 1/9
c. 11/90
d. 12/90
e. 13/90

Science

1. Which of the following substances allows for the fastest diffusion?
   a. Gas
   b. Solid
   c. Liquid
   d. Plasma

2. What is the oxidation number of hydrogen in CaH₂?
   a. +1
   b. –1
   c. 0
   d. +2

3. Which of the following does *not* exist as a diatomic molecule?
   a. Boron
   b. Fluorine
   c. Oxygen
   d. Nitrogen

4. What is another name for aqueous HI?
   a. Hydroiodate acid
   b. Hydrogen monoiodide
   c. Hydrogen iodide
   d. Hydriodic acid

5. What is the name for the reactant that is entirely consumed by the reaction?
   a. Limiting reactant
   b. Reducing agent
   c. Reaction intermediate
   d. Reagent

6. What is the name for the horizontal rows of the periodic table?
   a. Groups
   b. Periods
   c. Families
   d. Sets

7. What is the mass (in grams) of 7.35 mol water?
   a. 10.7 g
   b. 18 g
   c. 132 g
   d. 180.6 g

8. Which of the following orbitals is the last to fill?
   a. 1s
   b. 3s
   c. 4p
   d. 6s

9. What is the mass (in grams) of 1.0 mol oxygen gas?
    a. 12 g
    b. 16 g
    c. 28 g
    d. 32 g

10. Which kind of radiation has no charge?
    a. Beta
    b. Alpha
    c. Delta
    d. Gamma

11. What is the name of the state in which forward and reverse chemical reactions are occurring at the same rate?
    a. Equilibrium
    b. Constancy
    c. Stability
    d. Toxicity

12. What is 119°K in degrees Celsius?
    a. 32°C
    b. −154°C
    c. 154°C
    d. −32°C

13. What is the SI unit of energy?
    a. Ohm
    b. Joule
    c. Henry
    d. Newton

14. What is the name of the device that separates gaseous ions by their mass-to-charge ratio?
    a. Mass spectrometer
    b. Interferometer
    c. Magnetometer
    d. Capacitance meter

15. Which material has the smallest specific heat?
    a. Water
    b. Wood
    c. Aluminum
    d. Glass

16. What is the name for a reaction in which electrons are transferred from one atom to another?
    a. Combustion reaction
    b. Synthesis reaction
    c. Redox reaction
    d. Double-displacement reaction

17. What are van der Waals forces?
   a. The weak forces of attraction between two molecules
   b. The strong forces of attraction between two molecules
   c. Hydrogen bonds
   d. Conjugal bonds

18. What is the name for the number of protons in an atom?
   a. Atomic identity
   b. Atomic mass
   c. Atomic weight
   d. Atomic number

19. If an organism is *AaBb*, which of the following combinations in the gametes is impossible?
   a. AB
   b. aa
   c. aB
   d. Ab

20. How does water affect the temperature of a living thing?
   a. Water increases temperature.
   b. Water keeps temperature stable.
   c. Water decreases temperature.
   d. Water does not affect temperature.

21. What kind of bond connects sugar and phosphate in DNA?
   a. Hydrogen
   b. Ionic
   c. Covalent
   d. Overt

22. What is the second part of an organism's scientific name?
   a. Species
   b. Phylum
   c. Population
   d. Kingdom

23. How are lipids different than other organic molecules?
   a. They are indivisible.
   b. They are not water soluble.
   c. They contain zinc.
   d. They form long proteins.

24. Which of the following is *not* a steroid?
   a. Cholesterol
   b. Estrogen
   c. Testosterone
   d. Hemoglobin

25. Which hormone is produced by the pineal gland?
    a. Insulin
    b. Testosterone
    c. Melatonin
    d. Epinephrine

26. What is the name of the organelle that organizes protein synthesis?
    a. Mitochondrion
    b. Nucleus
    c. Ribosome
    d. Vacuole

27. What is the name for a cell that does *not* contain a nucleus?
    a. Eukaryote
    b. Bacteria
    c. Prokaryote
    d. Cancer

28. What is the name for the physical presentation of an organism's genes?
    a. Phenotype
    b. Species
    c. Phylum
    d. Genotype

29. Which of the following is *not* found within a bacterial cell?
    a. Mitochondria
    b. DNA
    c. Vesicles
    d. Ribosome

30. Which of the following is a protein?
    a. Cellulose
    b. Hemoglobin
    c. Estrogen
    d. ATP

31. Which of the following structures is *not* involved in translation?
    a. tRNA
    b. mRNA
    c. Ribosome
    d. DNA

32. How many different types of nucleotides are there in DNA?
    a. One
    b. Two
    c. Four
    d. Eight

33. Which of the following cell types has no nucleus?
   a. Platelet
   b. Red blood cell
   c. White blood cell
   d. Phagocyte

34. What is the name of the process by which a bacterial cell splits into two new cells?
   a. Mitosis
   b. Meiosis
   c. Replication
   d. Fission

35. What is the name of the structure that prevents food from entering the airway?
   a. Trachea
   b. Esophagus
   c. Diaphragm
   d. Epiglottis

36. What is the name of the outermost layer of skin?
   a. Dermis
   b. Epidermis
   c. Subcutaneous tissue
   d. Hypodermis

37. Which of the following structures has the lowest blood pressure?
   a. Arteries
   b. Arteriole
   c. Venule
   d. Vein

38. Which of the heart chambers is the most muscular?
   a. Left atrium
   b. Right atrium
   c. Left ventricle
   d. Right ventricle

39. Which part of the brain interprets sensory information?
   a. Cerebrum
   b. Hindbrain
   c. Cerebellum
   d. Medulla oblongata

40. How much air does an adult inhale in an average breath?
   a. 500 mL
   b. 750 mL
   c. 1000 mL
   d. 1250 mL

41. How much of a female's blood volume is composed of red blood cells?
   a. 10%
   b. 25%
   c. 40%
   d. 70%

Questions 42 and 43 are based on the following figures and text:

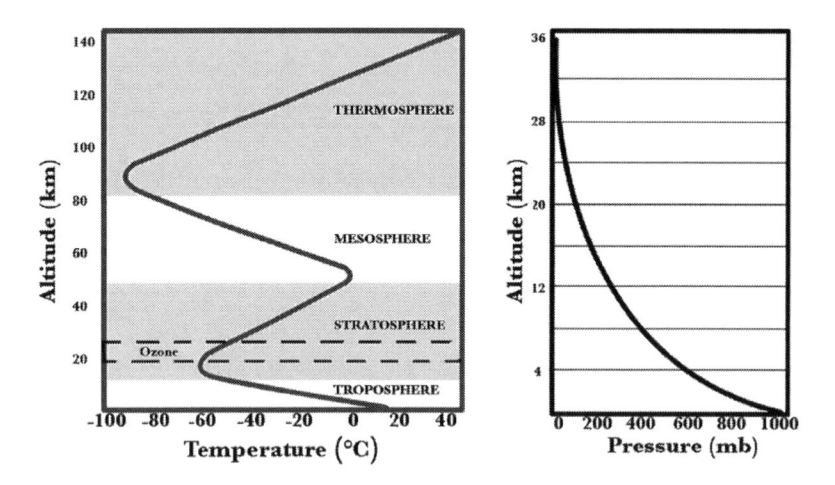

The Earth's atmosphere is comprised of multiple layers with very different temperature characteristics. Closest to the surface, the *troposphere* contains approximately 75 percent of the atmosphere's mass and 99 percent of its water vapor and aerosols. Temperature fluctuations cause constant mixing of air in the troposphere through convection, but it generally becomes cooler as altitude increases.

The *stratosphere* is heated by the absorption of ultraviolet radiation from the sun. Since its lower layers are composed of cooler, heavier air, there is no convective mixing in the stratosphere, and it is quite stable.

The *mesosphere* is the atmospheric layer directly above the stratosphere. Here, temperature decreases as altitude increases due to decreased solar heating and, to a degree, CO_2. In the lower atmosphere, CO_2 acts as a greenhouse gas by absorbing infrared radiation from the earth's surface. In the mesosphere, CO_2 cools the atmosphere by radiating heat into space.

Above this layer lies the *thermosphere*. At these altitudes, atmospheric gases form layers according to their molecular masses. Temperatures increase with altitude due to absorption of solar radiation by the small amount of residual oxygen. Temperatures are highly dependent on solar activity, and can rise to 1,500°C.

42. Commercial jetliners typically cruise at altitudes of 9-12 km, in the lower reaches of the stratosphere. Which of the following might be the reason for this choice of cruising altitude?
   a. Jet engines run more efficiently at colder temperatures.
   b. There is less air resistance than at lower altitudes.
   c. There is less turbulence than at lower altitudes.
   d. All of the above are possible reasons.

43. The lowest temperatures in the Earth's atmosphere are recorded within the

　　a. Troposphere
　　b. Stratosphere
　　c. Mesosphere
　　d. Thermosphere

44. A solar eclipse is

　　a. when the moon comes between the sun and the earth
　　b. the path of the sun across the celestial sphere
　　c. a geometrical curve
　　d. when the earth comes between the moon and the sun

45. Pollination involves which plant parts?

　　a. Xylem and petiole
　　b. Apical meristem and floral meristem
　　c. Anther and stigma
　　d. Root hairs and stroma

46. A scientist wants to measure the direction and duration of the movement of the ground. Which of the following instruments will the scientist most likely use?

　　a. A laser light with holograph
　　b. A seismograph
　　c. An electron microscope
　　d. A stereoscope

47. Most of the energy in a food chain is concentrated in the level of the

　　a. primary producers.
　　b. primary consumers.
　　c. secondary consumers.
　　d. tertiary consumers.

48. Which part of aerobic respiration uses oxygen?

　　a. Osmosis
　　b. Krebs cycle
　　c. Glycolysis
　　d. Electron transport system

49. Which of the following properties is responsible for the passage of water through a plant?

　　a. Cohesion
　　b. Adhesion
　　c. Osmosis
　　d. Evaporation

50. Which of the following is *not* a product of the Krebs cycle?

　　a. Carbon dioxide
　　b. Oxygen
　　c. Adenosine triphosphate (ATP)
　　d. Energy carriers

Social Studies

HISTORY

1. Which events are correctly paired to show cause and effect?

    a. the Spanish-American War → the U.S. annexation of Hawaii
    b. the assassination of William McKinley → the decline of U.S. imperialism
    c. the Russo-Japanese War → the Boxer Rebellion
    d. the Platt Amendment → the establishment of the U.S. naval base at Guantanamo Bay

2. Put the following events in order from oldest to most recent.

    1. Martin Luther King led the March on Washington.
    2. Brown v. Board of Education overturned the policy of "separate but equal" education.
    3. The Student Non-Violent Coordinating Committee began staging sit-ins at segregated lunch counters in the South.
    4. The arrest of Rosa Parks sparked the Montgomery Bus Boycott.

    a. 2,4,3,1
    b. 1,3,2,4
    c. 3,4,1,2
    d. 2,1,4,3

3. The annexation of Texas by the United States in 1845 was:

    a. an effort to help stem the spread of slavery west of the Mississippi.
    b. part of an effort to fulfill Manifest Destiny.
    c. an expression of principles set forth in the Monroe Doctrine.
    d. an effort to improve relations between the United States and Mexico.

4. The reforms set in motion by the Russian leader Mikhail Gorbachev played an important role in:

    a. the breakup of the Soviet Union.
    b. creating economic prosperity in post-Cold War Russia.
    c. prolonging the Cold War.
    d. ending the war in Bosnia.

5. Which of the following best describes the significance of the U.S. Supreme Court's decision in the Dred Scott case?

    a. The ruling effectively declared slavery to be a violation of the Constitution.
    b. The ruling guaranteed full citizenship rights to freed slaves.
    c. The ruling turned many Southerners against the Supreme Court.
    d. The ruling furthered the gap between North and South and hastened the Civil War.

6. The Sugar Act (1764), the Stamp Act (1765), and the Townshend Acts (1767-1770) all aroused the American colonists' concerns about:

    a. separation of powers.
    b. taxation without representation.
    c. the right to an impartial and speedy trial.
    d. freedom of speech.

7. Article I of the United States Constitution includes the following paragraph:

No title of nobility shall be granted by the United States: and no person holding any office of profit or trust under them, shall, without the consent of the Congress, accept of any present, emolument, office, or title, of any kind whatever, from any king, prince, or foreign state.

This paragraph most directly reflects the influence of:
 a. John Locke.
 b. Baron de Montesquieu.
 c. Jean-Jacques Rousseau.
 d. Thomas Paine.

8. Under the Articles of Confederation, Congress was not granted the power to:
 a. wage war and make treaties.
 b. regulate Indian affairs.
 c. appoint military officers.
 d. levy taxes.

9. Unlike slaves, who were considered to be the property of their masters, most indentured servants in colonial times:
 a. received wages for their labor.
 b. were generally treated kindly by their employers.
 c. were highly educated.
 d. voluntarily entered into servitude.

10. The main author of the Bill of Rights was:
 a. George Washington.
 b. John Adams.
 c. Thomas Jefferson.
 d. James Madison.

11. The first ships to set sail from Europe in the Age of Exploration departed from:
 a. Spain.
 b. the Netherlands.
 c. England.
 d. Portugal.

12. A book that influenced Congress to pass the Food and Drug Act of 1906 was:
 a. *The Octopus* by Frank Norris.
 b. *How the Other Half Lives* by Jacob Riis.
 c. *The Jungle* by Upton Sinclair.
 d. *The Shame of the Cities* by Lincoln Steffens.

13. The First Amendment to the Constitution deals mainly with:
 a. the right of free expression.
 b. the right to a speedy and public trial.
 c. protection from cruel and unusual punishment.
 d. freedom from unreasonable search and seizure.

14. The Federal Deposit Insurance Corporation (FDIC) and the Securities and Exchange Commission (SEC) were created during the presidency of:
   a. Theodore Roosevelt.
   b. Woodrow Wilson.
   c. Franklin Roosevelt.
   d. Harry Truman.

15. Which act of Parliament angered the American colonists without raising the issue of unfair taxation?
   a. the Sugar Act
   b. the Stamp Act
   c. The Quartering Act
   d. The Townshend Acts

16. The following lines were written by Paul Revere in 1770:

Unhappy Boston! See thy sons deplore

Thy hallowed walks besmear'd with guiltless gore.

While faithless Preston and his savage bands,

With murderous rancor stretch their bloody hands;

Like fierce barbarians grinning o'er their prey,

Approve the carnage and enjoy the day.

The event that inspired these words was:
   a. the Boston Massacre.
   b. the Boston Tea Party.
   c. the midnight ride of Paul Revere
   d. the Battle of Lexington and Concord

17. The principle that freedom of speech can be limited when the exercise of that freedom creates "a clear and present danger" was established in which Supreme Court decision?
   a. Plessy v. Ferguson (1896)
   b. Schenck v. United States (1919)
   c. Engle v. Vitale (1962)
   d. Miranda v. Arizona (1966)

18. The purpose of the Dayton Accords of 1995 was to resolve the bloody conflict in:
   a. Bosnia.
   b. Kosovo.
   c. Albania.
   d. Croatia.

19. In writing the sole dissenting opinion in a famous Supreme Court case, Justice John Marshall Harlan wrote these words:

> Our Constitution is color-blind, and neither knows nor tolerates classes among citizens. In respect of civil rights, all citizens are equal before the law.

The case about which he was writing was:

a. Marbury v. Madison.
b. Plessy v. Ferguson.
c. Gideon v. Wainwright.
d. Brown v. Board of Education.

20. Which of the following wars included no major army battles on American soil and no major changes in territories?

a. Queen Anne's War
b. King William's War
c. King George's War
d. The French and Indian War

ECONOMICS

1. An action's opportunity cost is best explained in terms of:

a. the minimum amount a business must borrow for the action.
b. the opportunities given up in order to pursue that action.
c. the percentage of one's overall budget that the action requires.
d. the cost of a long-term action adjusted for inflation.

2. The U.S. government seeks to reduce unemployment in part to prevent individuals from suffering hardship. How is unemployment also most likely to affect the economy?

a. By causing inflation
b. By leading to lost productivity
c. By increasing aggregate demand
d. By increasing aggregate supply

3. Consider the graph below. Which of the following is true?

a. The price has decreased with a shift in supply.
b. The equilibrium point has remained constant.
c. The price has risen with a shift in demand.
d. There a double coincidence of wants.

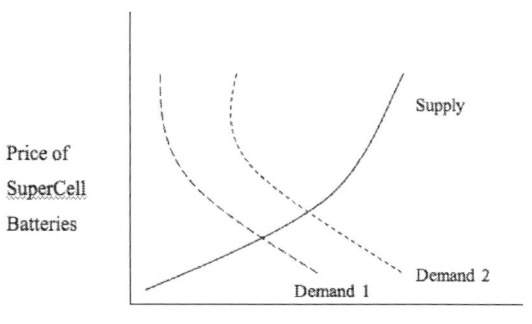

4. One reason for Jefferson's opposition to the Bank of the United States was that he:

a. did not think the Bank would effectively further his goal of establishing a strong central government.
b. was a strict constructionist.
c. believed the Bank would give an unfair advantage to the southern states.
d. distrusted the fiscal policies of the Democratic-Republicans.

5. A major cause of the Great Depression of the 1930s was:

a. the overproduction and underconsumption of consumer goods.
b. the failure of industry to produce sufficient consumer goods.
c. underproduction and rising prices in the agricultural sector.
d. the reduction of import tariffs.

6. An economist who advocated government intervention to prevent and remedy recessions and depressions was:

a. Adam Smith.
b. John Maynard Keynes.
c. Friedrich Hayek.
d. Milton Friedman.

7. The economist who focused on the potential for populations to grow faster than available food supplies was:

a. Adam Smith.
b. John Stuart Mill.
c. Thomas Malthus.
d. Friedrich Engels.

8. Under the United States Constitution, the power to tax and borrow is:

a. implied.
b. shared.
c. expressed.
d. reserved.

9. Which of the following is not correct regarding assumptions of mercantilism?

a. The money and the wealth of a nation are identical properties
b. In order to prosper, a nation should try to increase its imports
c. In order to prosper, a nation should try to increase its exports
d. Economic protectionism by national governments is advisable

10. The major role of the central bank of the United States, the Federal Reserve System, is...

a. To ensure that commercial bank reserves do not fall below levels set by Congress.
b. To advise the President on monetary policy and the state of the U.S. economy.
c. To promote full employment, price stability and economic growth.
d. To regulate long term monetary goals and contain inflation.

CIVICS AND GOVERNMENT

1. Which line of the chart below best lists the kinds of cases over which the U.S. federal court system has jurisdiction?

    a. Line 1
    b. Line 2
    c. Line 3
    d. Line 4

Jurisdiction of the Federal Court System

Line 1	Constitutional law	Bankruptcy	Most contract cases
Line 2	Constitutional law	Most contract cases	Most criminal cases
Line 3	Constitutional law	Bankruptcy	Disputes between states
Line 4	Constitutional law	Most personal injury cases	Disputes between states

2. Civic responsibility differs from personal responsibility in that the subject matter of civic responsibility is mainly:

    a. fair reporting of government actions.
    b. fair dealings between governments.
    c. a person's responsibilities as a citizen.
    d. a person's responsibilities as a government worker.

3. The concept of due process in the Fifth Amendment to the U.S. Constitution protects individuals by:

    a. guaranteeing a citizen's right to a trial by jury within a reasonable timeframe.
    b. restricting the government's ability to remove basic rights without following the law.
    c. guaranteeing a citizen's right to equal protection under the law.
    d. restricting the government's ability to remove basic rights without dire cause.

4. In the United States, the Electoral College elects the President and Vice President. The number of Electoral College members allowed to each state is equal to:

    a. the state's number of U.S. Representatives plus counties.
    b. the state's number of U.S. Senators plus Representatives.
    c. the state's number of U.S. Representatives plus state Secretaries.
    d. the state's number of U.S. Senators plus counties.

5. How does the executive branch of a parliamentary democracy differ from that in the United States' form of government?

    a. It appoints the legislative branch.
    b. It is a committee of the judicial branch.
    c. It is appointed by the judicial branch.
    d. It is a committee of the legislative branch.

6. Which of the following is the most frequently used tool of the Federal Reserve to control monetary policy?

a. Changing the interest rate at which banks can borrow from the Federal Reserve
b. Buying and selling stock options to raise or reduce interest rates
c. Adjusting the percentage of deposits a bank is required to keep on hand
d. Buying and selling government bonds to raise or reduce interest rates

7. A business can be a corporation, partnership, or sole proprietorship. For a business owner, what is one advantage of a running a corporation instead of a sole proprietorship?

a. Corporations offer limited liability protection.
b. Corporations avoid the "double tax" problem.
c. Corporations are more expensive to form.
d. Corporations are easier to dissolve.

8. The idea that the purpose of the American colonies was to provide Great Britain with raw materials and a market for its goods is an expression of:

a. free trade.
b. most favored nation status.
c. mercantilism.
d. laissez-faire capitalism.

9. Which of the following accurately describes the process by which government officials may be impeached and removed from office?

a. Charges are brought by the House of Representatives and tried in the Senate.
b. Charges are brought by the Senate and tried in the House of Representatives.
c. Charges are brought by the Attorney-General and tried in Congress.
d. Charges are brought by both houses of Congress and tried in the Supreme Court.

10. The power of the President to veto an act of Congress is an example of:

a. checks and balances.
b. separation of powers.
c. judicial review.
d. advice and consent

11. Congress can override the Presidential veto of a bill by:

a. a majority vote in the House and a two-thirds majority in the Senate.
b. a two-thirds vote in the House and a majority in the Senate.
c. a majority vote in both the House and the Senate.
d. a two-thirds vote in both the House and the Senate.

12. Which of the following is NOT an example of a shared, or concurrent, power?

a. the power to build roads
b. the power to coin money
c. the power to collect taxes
d. the power to establish courts

Geography

1. Which of these states was NOT one of the original 13 colonies?

   a. Maine
   b. Rhode Island
   c. New Hampshire
   d. New Jersey

2. Which biome is NOT found in the Torrid Zone?

   a. desert
   b. savanna
   c. rainforest
   d. taiga

3. The leading producers of petroleum in Latin America are:

   a. Argentina and Bolivia.
   b. Brazil and Guatemala.
   c. Mexico and Venezuela.
   d. Columbia and Uruguay.

4. The best map to use if you needed to find the highest elevation in a state would be a:

   a. political map.
   b. topographic map.
   c. resource map.
   d. road map.

5. The Tropic of Capricorn:

   a. separates the northern and southern hemispheres.
   b. separates the eastern and western hemispheres.
   c. is the southernmost latitude at which the sun can appear directly overhead at noon.
   d. is the northernmost latitude at which the sun can appear directly overhead at noon.

6. Which of the following was the first canal built in New York State?

   a. The Cayuga-Seneca Canal
   b. The Chambly Canal
   c. The Oswego Canal
   d. The Erie Canal

7. The Mojave Desert is located in which country?

   a. Afghanistan
   b. Morocco
   c. Australia
   d. United States

8. Approximately what percentage of the Earth's surface is land?

   a. 50
   b. 10
   c. 30
   d. 85

Answer Key and Explanations

Language Arts - Reading

1. C: A stanza consists of a grouping of lines, set off by a space, that usually has a set pattern of meter and rhyme. This poem has six stanzas.

2. E: Personification is a metaphor in which a thing or abstraction is represented as a person. Personification is used throughout this poem. However, of the answer choices given, line 11 is the best choice. The author personifies spring as a female.

3. A: The fifth stanza gives clues to whom "we" refers.

"Not one would mind, neither bird nor tree

If mankind perished utterly"

"We" is referencing mankind, choice (A).

4. B: This is an example of a rhymed verse poem. The last two words of each line rhymes in every stanza. A sonnet is a poem of fourteen lines following a set rhyme scheme and logical structure. Often, poets use iambic pentameter when writing sonnets. A free verse poem is written without using strict meter or rhyme. A lyric poem is a short poem that expresses personal feelings, which may or may not be set to music. An epic poem is a long narrative poem, usually about a serious subject. It often contains details of heroic deeds and events significant to a culture or nation.

5. A: Answer choice A gives the best summary of the poem, demonstrated by the phrases about things in nature not caring about war or the extinction of humanity.

6. D: The first paragraph gives the information to correctly answer this question.

7. B: This passage in arranged by problem and solution. The author states a problem that the cotton farmers were having: "Eventually, cotton will no longer grow on this land." The author then presents a solution: "Carver told farmers to rotate their crops: plant cotton one year, then the next year plant peanuts and other soil-restoring plants, like peas and sweet potatoes. It worked! The peanut plants grew and produced lots of peanuts."

8. E: The second paragraph discusses the problem the cotton farmers were facing. The cotton crops had depleted the nutrients from the soil.

9. A: The last paragraph answers this question. "Carver told farmers to rotate their crops: plant cotton one year, then the next year plant peanuts and other soil-restoring plants, like peas and sweet potatoes. It worked! The peanut plants grew and produced lots of peanuts."

10. C: Answer choice (C) best summarizes what this passage is mainly about. Choices (A), (B), and (C) are not even discussed in this passage. Paragraph 5 does discuss choice (E), but it is not the main focus of the passage.

11. A: Answer choice (A) best defines "crop rotation." The passage gives the definition in the last paragraph.

12. B: As set out in section 1.0, Purpose and Scope, the document describes a procedure for identifying hazards associated with one or more jobs (in this case Tank Operations) or encountered by visitors and for instituting controls to mitigate (or minimize) the dangers that they present.

13. D: The methods to be used to mitigate hazards are given in section 4.1 of the text, which indicates that they are specified in descending order of use. Protective clothing is an example of the last method listed, personal protective equipment, so this is the last strategy to be tried to protect the workers from the hazardous chemical.

14. D: Section 4.2 indicates that safety procedures ("controls") that fall within the scope of normal training for workers do not need to be discussed in the work instructions for operations that are performed frequently.

15. A: The document is intended as a guide for those writing work instructions for jobs to be performed at the site. These work instructions are prepared by management. Workers and laborers would read those documents as part of their training.

16. D: Section 4.5 indicates that safety procedures that are not within the qualification and training of the workers for hazards should have detailed instructions for how the workers are to mitigate the hazard.

17. B: The extract includes a number of plays on words, exaggerations, and other comic devices that show that it is meant to be funny.

18. C: As part of their argument, the Doctor and Martine are regretting that they are married to one another. As a result, she regrets the day that she said "yes, and, in the very next line, he regrets having signed the marriage papers.

19. A: In this section, Martine levels a series of accusations at the Doctor: drinking, selling the furniture, gambling. His answers are all flippant one-liners that mock her and that show no regret. Nor does he attempt to defend his actions in any way.

20. C: The Doctor drinks, gambles, sells all that they own and takes no responsibility for the children. He does not appear to be irascible or choleric (both indicate someone who is easily angered) or intolerant (someone who does not respect other beliefs or opinions).

21. D: In this portion of the extract, the Doctor tells Martine to be gentle and, backing away, tells her not to get into a passion, that is, to become emotional. He tries to placate her and then, in the last line, stands his ground and becomes combative as well.

22. C: The passage makes no mention of metals or horses. Although we may infer that they hunted the buffalo because they were plentiful, that is not stated in the passage.

23. B: Travail means work, or effort, and shows that the crows made it more difficult for the people to kill buffalo during the hunt.

24. B: The story tells us that after the great white crow turned black, all the other crows were black as well. Thus, he is a symbol for all these birds.

25. D: Line 18 tells us that the tribe planned to frighten the chief of the crows to prevent the crows from warning the buffalo about the hunts. The passage does not suggest that they hated all birds or that they planned to eat this one.

26. C: Long Arrow acted like the buffalo in the herd so that the chief of the crows would approach, making it possible to capture him. Although we may infer that he had to fool the buffalo in the herd as well, this is secondary to his need to fool the birds.

27. B: These details help us to see how the people lived. Although they hunted with the stone tipped spears, the rawhide bag was not a part of the hunt.

28. A: As he lands, he asks "have you not heard my warning?" (Line 41).

29. A: The suggestions included several for killing or mutilating the bird, which does not suggest a calm resolve. And there is no suggestion that they were either celebrating or hungry at this time.

30. D: There is no characterization of Long Arrow in the passage, and we know nothing

About him or why he was chosen.

31. B: The birds in the story are able to observe the actions of hunters, to interpret them as potentially harmful for their buffalo friends, and to act for the protection of the buffalo. They do not appear to do this for their own benefit, nor do they seem to act specifically to harm the tribe, but rather to help the buffalo.

32. B: Gorkhi is described in line 6 as a bit bombastic. A bombastic individual is one who is overbearing and pretentious.

33. D: Line 13 tells us that Zakov found the student on the floor.

34. D: Nasadev is described as whining, with his eyes red from crying, and concerned that his troubles will affect his family.

35. C: Zakov tries to understand how the student must have felt about Olga's rejection. His "heart went out" to the student, and later, when he leaves, he feels a deep sadness for him.

36. A: The student regards Zakov with an imploring look. To implore is to beg.

37. B: The passage describes his voice as "practically inaudible", which means "unable to be heard", but does not describe it as a whisper.

38. C: Olga's rejection of the student provides a reasonable motive, but there is nothing in the passage to suggest that Zakov had proof of Nasadev's guilt or innocence.

39. D: The passage describes Hal as a very large man suited to contact sports, and this metaphor indicates that he had massive legs the size of tree trunks.

40. B: Cats are known to move very quietly. Here, Hal's massive size is being contrasted with his ability to move as quietly as a cat.

Language Arts - Writing

1. B: This sentence uses the correct pronoun "who" to refer to the caregivers, who are people and not things. Choices A and D respectively use "that" and "which," both of which are pronouns used to refer to things and not people. Choice C has a misused comma after "spouses." Choice E incorrectly uses the objective pronoun "whom."

2. E: This choice is correct because it uses a semicolon with the connecting word "however." Choice A incorrectly uses a comma between the two independent phrases. Choice B uses an incorrect plural form of "support," which is an adjective. Choice C has a singular "service" with the plural verb "are." Choice D is a run-on sentence.

3. C: This choice is correct because it uses the adverb "then." Choice A incorrectly uses the conjunction "than." Choice B incorrectly uses a semicolon after "journey," which creates incomplete phrases. Choice D incorrectly omits the apostrophe indicating possession in "one's." And choice E uses the wrong tense of the helping verb "have."

4. C: This choice is correct because it uses the comma after "age" in the introductory phrase. Choice A lacks the comma. Choice B incorrectly uses plurals for "day," "age" and "this." Choice D uses the incorrect preposition "from." Choice E is incorrect because it uses a singular verb while "options" is plural.

5. C: By combining the sentences and eliminating unnecessary words, the two sentences express the same idea, but are clearer and more succinct. Choice A is correct grammatically, but it is redundant and has too many extra words. Choice B uses a semicolon incorrectly. Both choices D and E are easy to misunderstand and use semicolons where question marks would be more appropriate.

6. A: This choice is correct because it uses the adverb "how," while choices B and C incorrectly use the adverbs "where" and "when," respectively. Choice D has the wrong verb tense with "knew." Choice E uses "to" instead of "they," removing a necessary subject.

7. C: This choice is correct because both verbs agree. Choice A is not correct because "have" does not agree with the first verb, "having." Although the correct verbs are used in choice B, it still is incorrect because the singular article "a" should not be used with the plural noun "detectors." Choice D incorrectly omits the article "a" before "emergency supply kit." Choice E incorrectly uses a semicolon, although the verb choices are correct.

8. A: A comma is the best punctuation after "days." Choice B uses a semicolon incorrectly. Choice C uses the incorrect conjunction "which." Choice D is not correct because it uses a possessive form of "days," which is not required. Choice E incorrectly uses the contraction "you've" together with "have."

9. B: This choice is correct because it uses commas to set off a phrase. Choice A omits the comma after "rotate." Choice C uses a comma after "Remember" where it is not needed. Choice D uses no commas at all, which is not correct. Choice E inserts a comma after "insulin" where it is not needed.

10. C: This choice uses the correct flow of ideas. Choice A incorrectly separates the idea of storing from "per person per day." Choice B is awkward and almost incomprehensible. Choice D incorrectly uses a comma after "day." Choice E, does not read well.

11. E: No capitals are necessary for the words "warm," "weather" or "climate" because they are not proper nouns or geographical names. Choices A and D are not correct because they capitalize words that do not need to be capitalized. Choice B incorrectly uses the comparative form of "warmer." Choice C is not correct because it does not have a comma after the opening phrase.

12. D: Choice D follows the theme of preparedness in the passage. Choice A is not a complete sentence. Choice B is incorrect because the pronouns "you" and "we" do not agree. Choice C is not correct because it has nothing to do with the ideas presented in the first 12 sentences. Choice E is incorrect because it simply repeats the first half of sentence 6.

13. C: This choice is correct because it uses a comma before "but" and after "which" so that the ideas are combined. Choice A incorrectly uses a comma after "drugs" and also has a possessive form of the noun "germs." Choice B has a comma before "this is called resistance" where a semicolon is needed. Choice D has an incorrect verb form in "resists." Choice E has the plural subject "drugs" with the singular verb "saves," making it incorrect as well.

14. B: The correct choice uses "as" to indicate a degree. Choice A incorrectly uses "even," which indicates a greater degree. Choice C uses the comparative "better," even though there is no comparison. Choice D is improper use of the English language. Choice E uses a double negative.

15. E: Choice E is correct because it uses "antibiotics" as a group with the plural verb "work." Choice A would be correct if used with the article "an" and a singular verb. Choice B uses the incorrect preposition "with." Choice C incorrectly adds an "s" to "bacteria" when the word is already plural. Choice D uses an apostrophe with "antibiotic's" when there is no possession.

16. E: Choice E correctly uses two clauses connected by a comma. Choice A omits the second "the" before "likely," resulting in awkward phrasing. Choice B contains two incomplete sentences. Choice C uses two comparatives; it should be either "more likely" or "likelier," but not both. Choice D uses "oftener," which is not a word.

17. B: There are two statements, and "In fact" serves as a connector, so it should be followed by a comma. Choice A incorrectly runs the two together into one sentence. By putting "in fact" at the end of the first sentence, choice C makes little sense. Choice D is a run-on sentence. And Choice E forms an incorrect contraction of "will not."

18. C: This choice logically follows the two previous sentences. Choice A is not a complete sentence. Although Choices B, D and E could be true, they do not have anything to do with the content of the passage.

19. D: The correct verb form is "need," not "needing." In choice A, "needing" is an incorrect verb form because it is a participle that is not called for here. Choice B does not use the infinitive and is incorrect. Choice C has an incorrect form of the verb "be." Choice E incorrectly uses the infinitive of "need."

20. E: The words "for example" suggest that a specific example is about to be stated. Choices A and B do not have the correct relationship, nor do choices C and D.

21. E: Choice E is correct because it inserts the phrase "such as" to mean "for example," which completes the thought. In choice A, the second sentence is incomplete because it has no verb. Putting a period after "hours" also makes the second sentence incomplete in choice B. Choice C uses a semicolon incorrectly. In choice D, the sentence is a run-on and, by not putting a comma after "child," makes it look like the child is working long hours.

22. A: Choice A is correct because it uses the preposition "like" to mean "similar to." Choices B and C both use verbs that have no meaning in the context of the sentence. In choice D, "until" is an incorrect preposition meaning "up to the time of." Choice E incorrectly uses "likely" as an adverb, meaning "probably."

23. C: The only capital letter in the sentence should be the letter beginning the sentence. Choices A, B and D all have words which are incorrectly capitalized. Choice E incorrectly uses the conjunction "but," meaning "except," which makes no sense.

24. C: Sentence 17 talks about medicine and choice C is a logical next thought. Choice A does not follow as a logical next idea. Choices B and D have nothing in common with any part of the passage. Choice E is not a complete sentence.

25. D: The article "a" is used before a consonant. Choice A incorrectly uses "an," which should be used before a vowel. Choice B incorrectly uses the conjunction "and" instead of an article. Choice C places a comma where none is required. Choice E incorrectly uses the singular article "a" with the plural noun "diets."

26. D: "Includes" and "can contribute" are both in the present tense. Choice A is not correct because "included" is in the past tense. Choice B uses a semicolon incorrectly. Choice C has the preposition "than" instead of the pronoun "that." Choice E is incorrect because a comma is needed before the pronoun "which."

27. E: This choice uses the contraction "it's" for "it is." Choice A incorrectly uses the possessive pronoun "its." Choice B does not have an infinitive, but an incorrect participle for the verb. Choice C uses the incorrect adverb "importantly" rather than the adjective "important." And in choice D, the adjective "safe" is incorrectly used in place of the adverb "safely."

28. B: The colon is used to indicate the existence of a second clause. Choice A is incorrect because it capitalizes the word after the colon. Choice C is incorrect because "ask yourself" is not a sentence. Choice D is a run-on sentence, and choice E incorrectly uses a comma rather than a colon to separate the clauses.

29. A: This choice has the correct form of verb and adjective. Choice B is incorrect because "being sure" is not a complete statement. Choice C is not correct because the verb "preserve" should be the adjective "preserved." Choice D incorrectly uses the participle "preserving." Choice E incorrectly uses the verb "buying" instead of "buy."

30. C: This choice follows logically from the information in the previous sentences. Choice A might be true, but has nothing to do with the passage. Choice B is an incomplete sentence. Choices D and choice E also do not really follow the main idea of the passage, which is buying seafood safely.

31. A: This sentence follows the ideas logically. Choices B and E are awkwardly written, and choices C and D do not make sense.

32. A: The words "in fact" show that an example is following. Choices B, D and E show the opposite or a contrast. Choice C does not make sense.

33. E: Choice E is correct because it replaces the possessive "their" with the adverb "there." Choice A uses the incorrect possessive form of "their." Choice B not only has the incorrect "their" but also has an incorrect verb form: it is plural and should be singular. Choice C uses a singular verb "is" when it should use the plural "are" to match "occupants." Choice D incorrectly inserts a comma where none is needed.

34. A: Choice B has an incorrect verb form while choice B incorrectly places a semicolon between two dependent clauses. Choice D incorrectly inserts a comma where none is needed. Choice E uses the incorrect verb form "occurs."

35. B: This choice uses the correct joining word "because," which indicates a cause and effect relationship. Choice A uses the word "although," which indicates contrast and not cause and effect. Choice C uses an incorrect transition phrase and, like choices D and E, does not make sense.

36. B: This choice follows the main idea of the passage. Choice A is true, but it is just another fact and not a logical conclusion to the passage. Similarly, choices C and D are interesting facts, but neither are logical conclusions to the passage. Choice E has nothing to do with the passage.

37. A: This choice has the correct order of thoughts. Choices B, C and D do not make sense. Choice E changes the meaning of the sentence.

38. C: The semicolon in this choice joins two independent clauses. Choice A is a run-on sentence. Choice B incorrectly uses a comma to join the two ideas. Choice D places a semicolon in the wrong place. Choice E inserts the transition word "although," which does not make sense in the context of the sentence.

39. B: This is the logical choice to go after sentence 7. Choice A is not related to the subject, although it is true. Choice C contradicts the passage. Choice D doesn't relate to the topic. Choice E is not relevant at all.

40. D: Choice D uses the correct verb form and agrees with "companies," the subject of the sentence. Choice A has an incorrect participle without a helping verb. Choice B has a singular helping verb where a plural is needed. Choice C also has an incorrect helping verb. Choice E has an incorrect verb form and doesn't agree with the subject.

41. A: This choice has the proper past tense of the verb "to order." Choice B has a possessive form of the noun "reviews," which is incorrect. Choice C has an incorrect verb form: it should be "ordered," not "order." Choice D inserts the word "even" and causes the sentence to not make sense. Choice E has an incorrect verb form.

42. E: "Finally" indicates the last thing that should be done in a series of items. Choice A suggests a cause and effect relationship which does not exist. Choice B does the same. Choices C and D do not make sense in the context of the sentence.

43. B: This choice changes the adjective "significant" to the adverb form so that it can modify the verb "increased." Choice A has an incorrect adjective modifying the verb. Choice C has the correct adverbial form, but does not have a comma after the opening phrase. Choice D changes the verb to a noun, which could have the adjective "significant," but the verb form is not correct. Choice E has both the incorrect adjective form and an incorrect verb as well.

44. A: The ideas in this choice follow in a logical order. Choice B says the exact opposite of what is meant. Choice C does not make sense. Choices D and E are awkwardly written.

45. E: The context of the sentence calls for a negative word. Choice A is incorrect. Choices B and C suggest a difference from the previous sentence, but there is none. Choice D does not make sense.

46. C: A semicolon has been correctly inserted between the two independent thoughts in choice C. Choice A is a run-on sentence. Choice B is incorrect because a comma was incorrectly used to separate two independent sentences. Choice D would be correct, except the verb from "make" does not agree with the subject "spending." Choice E is a run-on sentence, and the comma needed after "however" is incorrectly omitted.

47. E: This choice has changed the possessive form of "vegetables" to a non-possessive form. Choice A has the possessive form of "vegetables," which is incorrect. Choice B has the correct form for "vegetables," but a semicolon has been inserted incorrectly after "friend." Choice C has an incorrect verb form, "ordering." Choice D incorrectly makes "entrée" a plural noun, which does not agree with the article "an."

48. D: Choice D is another suggestion for how to not eat so much at fast food restaurants, meaning it follows the logic of the paragraph. Choice A has nothing to do with the topic. Choice B tells information that has already been stated in the passage. Choice C is an interesting detail, but does not fit within the context of the paragraph. Choice E is also an opinion that does not fit with the paragraph.

49. E: This choice fits in with the flow of the paragraph, while the others do not. Choice A is a fact that doesn't really belong in the paragraph. Choice B is information that was detailed earlier in the passage. Choice C is an opinion that doesn't have a place in a factual passage, and choice D is not relevant to the topic.

50. A: This is the only choice that makes sense with the logic of the paragraph. Choices B, D and E suggest something opposite to the prior sentence. Choice C does not make sense in the context of the passage.

Mathematics

1. C: Prime numbers are those that are only evenly divisible by one and themselves.

2. D: Multiply 30 by 0.2 and subtract this from the original price of the shirt to find the sale price: $24. Then multiply 24 by 0.2 and add the product to the sale price to find the final price.

3. C: There are 12 inches in a foot and 3 feet in a yard. Four and a half yards is equal to 162 inches. To determine the number of 3-inch segments, divide 162 by 3.

4. A: If it takes 3 people 3 1/3 days to do the job, then it would take one person 10 days: $3 \times 3\frac{1}{3} = 10$. Thus, it would take 2 people 5 days, and one day of work for two people would complete 1/5 of the job.

5. C: $10\sqrt{6} \neq 6\sqrt{10}$.

$$36 = 6^2 \neq 6\sqrt{10}$$

$$\sqrt{600} = \sqrt{6 \cdot 100} = 10\sqrt{6} \neq 6\sqrt{10}$$

$$\sqrt{6} \neq 6\sqrt{10}$$

$$10\sqrt{6} \neq 6\sqrt{10}$$

6. C: 16.5 x 4/3 = 22.

$$16.5 \times 4/3 \neq 10$$

$$16.5 \times 4/3 \neq 50$$

$$16.5 \times 4/3 \neq 18$$

$$16.5 \times 4/3 \neq 16.5$$

$$B/A = \tan(30°)$$

7. E: The fraction of those playing drums plus the fraction of those playing a brass instrument must total 1. So the number that play drums is *pn*, and the number playing brass must be (1-*p*)*n*.

A. $pn - 1$ is one less than the number playing drums.

B. $p(n - 1)$ applies the proportion to fewer than the total number of musicians.

C. $(p - 1)n$ results in a negative number (since *p* must be less than 1).

D. $(p + 1)n$ will be a number greater than the total number of musicians.

8. A: This is a right triangle, since the two angles shown add up to 90 degrees, and the remaining angle must therefore be 90 degrees. For a right triangle, the length of a side is related to the hypotenuse by the sine of the opposite angle. Thus $B = C \sin(30°)$ and since the sine of a 30-degree angle is 0.5, $B = C/2$.

B. *B* is related to *A* by the tangent of 30 degrees, which is greater than ½.

C.-E. All of these values are greater than B, since the hypotenuse, *C*, must be the longest side, and since *A* must be greater than *B*, since $B/A = \tan(30°)$, and the tangent of an angle less than 45 degrees will be less than 1.

9. D: Distance is the product of velocity and time, $(5 \times 10^6) \times 2 \times 10^{-4} = (10 \times 10^6 \times 10^{-4} = 10^3 = 1000$.

A. $50 \neq (5 \times 10^6) \times 2 \times 10^{-4}$

B. $25 \neq (5 \times 10^6) \times 2 \times 10^{-4}$

C. $100 \neq (5 \times 10^6) \times 2 \times 10^{-4}$

E. $200 \neq (5 \times 10^{6)} \times 2 \times 10^{-4}$

10. 24: First solve for b. If 3a + 5b = 98 and a = 11, then b = 13. Therefore, a + b is 11 + 13. The final answer is 24.

11. A: Since the second line, $y = 3$, is a vertical, the intersection must occur at a point where $y = 3$. If $x = -1.5$, the equation describing the line is satisfied: $2 \times [-1.5] + 3 = 0$
B. The equation for the first line is not satisfied: $(2 \times 1.5) + 3 \neq 0$

C-E. None of these points satisfy the condition y = 3, and thus they will not be traversed by the second line.

12. A: For the line to be parallel to the x-axis, the slope must be 0. This condition is met if y has a constant value.

B-D. y varies with x for all of these, and is therefore not parallel to the x-axis.

E is not correct, since A is a solution.

13. 30: The answer is found by dividing the volume of the rectangle (15 x 9 x 6) by the volume of the square (3 x 3 x 3). 810 divided by 27 is 30.

14. B: 25% off is equivalent to $25 \times \frac{\$138}{100} = \$34.50$, so the sale price becomes $138 - $34.50 = $103.50.

A. $67 ≠ $103.50

C. $34.50 is the amount of the reduction, not the final price.

D. $113 ≠ $103.50

E. $ 125 ≠ 103.50

15. A: The vertical operators indicate absolute values, which are always positive. Thus, $|7 - 5| = 2$, and $|7 - 5|=|-2|=2$, and $2 - 2 = 0$.

No other answer is correct because the answer is unique.

16. 35: A rectangle's area is length times width. Here, length is 5x and width is x so $5x^2 = 245$ and $x^2 = 49$. Therefore, x = 7 and the longest side is 35 inches.

17. B: The value of the fraction $\frac{7}{5}$ can be evaluated by dividing 7 by 5, which yields 1.4. The average of 1.4 and 1.4 is $\frac{1.4+1.4}{2} = 1.4$.

Answers A, C, and D are incorrect because the solution to a numeric equation is unique.

E is incorrect because B provides the correct answer.

18. C: The surface of a cube is obtained by multiplying the area of each face by 6, since there are 6 faces. The area of each face is the square of the length of one edge. Therefore $A = 6 \times 3^2 = 6 \times 9 = 54$.

Answers A, B, D, and E are incorrect since the surface area is a unique value.

19. 8: Rate = distance/time. Distance is 14. Time is 1 hour and 45 minutes, or $1\frac{3}{4}$, or 7/4. $\frac{14}{\frac{7}{4}} = 14 \times \frac{4}{7} = 8$.

20. A: The area A of a circle is given by $A = \pi \times r^2$, where r is the radius. Since π is approximately 3.14, we can solve for $r = \sqrt{\frac{A}{\pi}} = \sqrt{\frac{314}{3.14}} = \sqrt{100} = 10$. Now, the diameter d is twice the radius, or d = 2 x 10 = 20.

B. 10 is the value of the radius, not the diameter.

C, D, and E are all wrong as they do not equal 20.

21. D: Inspection of the data shows that the distance traveled by the car during any 1-unit interval (velocity) is 20 units. However, the first data point shows that the car is 50 units from the point of origin at time 2, so it had a 10-unit head start before time measurement began.

Answers A-C only fit the data at single points. They do not fit the whole set.

Answer E is incorrect since answer D fits all the data.

22. 16: To solve this problem, first set up the equation: (4 + 7 + 9 + x)/4 = 9. Multiply both sides by four to solve: 20 + x = 36. Therefore, x = 16.

23. A: The perimeter of a circle is given by $2\pi r$, where r is the radius. We solve for $r = \frac{35}{2\pi} = 5.57$, and double this value to obtain the diameter d = 11.14 feet.

Since this value is unique, all the other answers are incorrect. Answer C is the radius, not the diameter.

24. 25: If the ratio of pennies to nickels is 2:6, the ratio of the pennies to the combined coins is 2:2+6, or 2:8. This is ¼ or, expressed as a percentage, 25%.

25. 8: The largest prime factor of 42 is 7 and the smallest is 1. The sum of the two is 8.

26. C: Since 4 is the same as 2^2, $4^6 = 2^{12}$. When dividing exponents with the same base, simply subtract the exponent in the denominator from the exponent in the numerator.

27. B: Substitute the given values and solve. Resolve the parenthetical operations first.

28. A: Convert 20% to the fraction 1/5, then multiply by 12/5. The resulting fraction, 12/25, must have both numerator and denominator multiplied by 4 to become a percentage.

29. C: The expression 2^{-3} is equivalent to $\frac{1}{2^3}$, and since $2^3 = 8$, it is equivalent to 1/8.

A. $\frac{1}{4} = 2^{-2}$

B. $\frac{1}{12} \neq \frac{1}{8}$

D. $\frac{1}{16} = 2^{-4}$

E. $\frac{1}{12} \neq \frac{1}{8}$

30. 5: Use long division to determine how many times 12 goes into 137 (11 times) and see what remains. There is a remainder of 5.

31. D: The radius r of this circle is the line OA. Since B is a right angle, OA is the hypotenuse and by the Pythagorean theorem, $r^2 = x^2 + y^2$ so that $r = \sqrt{x^2 + y^2}$.

A. This is the simple sum of the segments and does not define r.

B. This is the square of the radius. The square root is required.

C and E contain constants (1 and 4) that are not related to the diagram and are therefore incorrect. E will be correct only where $y = 1$.

32. E: If segment AB equals segment OB, then the tangent of the angle AOB must be 1 ($\tan AOB$) = $\frac{AB}{OB} = 1$, which is the tangent of a 45 degree angle. Further, since AOB is a right triangle with angle ABO = 90 degrees, and since the sum of the angles in a triangle must equal 180 degrees, angle BAO must also be 45 degrees (45+45+90=180).

Therefore, A and B are both correct, and C is incorrect, since 90 ≠ 45. D is also an incorrect answer, since C is wrong.

33. A: Since both OA and OC are radii of the same circle, they must be equal.

B. Since AOB is a 45-degree angle, OB > BC

C. OB is a part of OC and therefore must be smaller. They cannot be equal.

D. Since AB = OB and OC > OB, then OC > AB

E. This is incorrect since A is true.

34. E: Each hour has 60 minutes, and each of those minutes has 60 seconds. Expressed in seconds, then, an hour is 60 x 60 = 3600. 400/3600 = 1/9.

35. 55: Larry gave away ¼ + 1/5 = 5/20 + 4/20 = 9/20 of his candy, so he had 11/20 left. 11/20 = 55/100 = 55%.

36. A: As defined, the line will be described by the equation $y = 4x + 1$. Expression A fits this equation ($9 = 4 \times 2 + 1$). The others do not.
B. $-1 \neq 4 \times 0 + 1$
C. $0 \neq 4 \times 0 + 1$
D. $4 \neq 4 \times 1 + 1$
E $1 \neq 4 \times 1 + 4$

37. B: 30% 0f 3300 = 0.3 x 3300 = 990

A. 330 is $\frac{330}{3300} \times 100 = 10\%$ of 3300, not 30%

C. 700 is $\frac{700}{3300} \times 100 = 21.2\%$ of 3300, not 30%

D. 1100 is $\frac{1100}{3300} \times 100 = 33.3\%$ of 3300, not 30%

E. 2310 is $\frac{2310}{3310} \times 100 = 70\%$ of 3300, not 30%

38. E: The sum of angles in a triangle equals 180 degrees. Therefore solve for the remaining angle as 180 – (15 + 70) = 95 degrees. Since this value is unique, all other answers are incorrect.

39. 75: 18 people did not complete the climb. 18/24 = ¾ = 75%.

40. B: This answer may be determined using the Law of Sines, which relates the sides of a triangle and their opposing angles as follows:

$$\frac{a}{\sin A} = \frac{b}{\sin B} = \frac{c}{\sin C}$$

Thus, we have $\sin A = a \times \frac{\sin B}{b} = 14 \times \frac{\sin(35)}{12} = 14 \times \frac{0.57}{12} = 0.67$, and

$$\sin^{-1}(0.67) = 42\ degrees.$$

Since this value is unique, all other answers are incorrect.

41. B: The inequality specifies that the difference between L and 15 inches must be less or equal to 0.01. For choice B, | 14.99 – 15 | = | -0.01 | = 0.01, which is equal to the specified tolerance and therefore meets the condition.

|14.9 – 15 | = | - 0.1 | = 0.1 which is greater than 0.01.

and D. are both longer than the length L and therefore not the minimum length.

14. 991 is within the acceptable tolerance range, but is longer than 14.99.

42. E: The product of x and $\frac{1}{x}$ is $\frac{1}{x} \times x = \frac{x}{x} = 1$ The expression x^{-1} is equivalent to $\frac{1}{x}$. Thus, both B and C are correct.

A. $(x - 1) \times x = x^2 - x \neq 1$

43. C: The total distance traveled was 8 + 3.6 = 11.6 miles. The first 1/5th of a mile is charged at the higher rate. Since 1/5th = 0.2, the remainder of the trip is 11.4 miles. Thus, the fare for the distance traveled is computed as $5.50 + 5 × 11.4 × $1.50 = $91. To this the charge for waiting time must be added, which is simply 9 x 20¢ = 180¢ = $1.80. Finally, add the two charges, $91 + $1.80 = $92.80. Since this value is unique, all other answers are incorrect.

44. E: Each term of each expression in parentheses must be multiplied by each term in the other. Thus, for E, $(x + 3)(3x - 5) = 3x^2 + 9x - 5x - 15 = 3x^2 + 4x - 15$

A. $(x - 3)(x + 5) = x^2 - 3x + 5x - 15 = x^2 + 2x - 15 \neq 3x^2 + 4x - 15$

B. $(x + 5)(3 + x) = 3x + 15 + x^3 + 5x^2 \neq 3x^2 + 4x - 15$

C. $x(3x + 4 - 15) = 3x^2 + 4x - 15x = 3x^2 - 11x \neq 3x^2 + 4x - 15$

D. $(3x^2 + 5)(3x - 5) = (9x^3 + 15x - 5x^2 - 25) \neq 3x^2 + 4x - 15$

45. C: Distance = rate x time. Here, Roxana's rate was 4 mph, and her time was 1.5 hours. Distance, therefore, is 6 miles. To determine how long it took Roxana to return, we solve the formula for time: 6 miles = 5mph x time. Distance/rate = 1 1/5 hours, or 72 minutes.

46. B: The probability of playing a song by any band is proportional to the number of songs by that band over the total number of songs, or $\frac{5}{15} = \frac{1}{3}$ for Band D. The probability of playing any particular song is not affected by what has been played previously, since the choice is random. Since this value is unique, answers A, C, and D are incorrect. E. is incorrect since the answer can be computed as shown.

47. A: Since 3 of the 15 songs are by Band B, the probability that any one song will be by that band is $\frac{3}{15} = \frac{1}{5}$. The probability that two successive events will occur is the product of the probabilities for any one event or, in this case $\frac{1}{5} \times \frac{1}{5} = \frac{1}{25}$. Since this value is unique, answers A, C, and D are incorrect. E. is incorrect since the answer can be computed as shown.

48. A: From the starting expression, compute: $3\left(\frac{6x-3}{3}\right) - 3(9x + 9) = 3(2x - 1) - 27x - 27 = 6x - 3 - 27x - 27 = -21x - 30 = -3(7x + 10)$

B. $-3x + 6 \neq 3\left(\frac{6x-3}{3}\right) - 3(9x + 9)$

C. $(x + 3)(x - 3) = x^2 + 3x - 3x - 9 = x^2 - 9 \neq 3\left(\frac{6x-3}{3}\right) - 3(9x + 9)$

D. $3x^2 - 9 \neq 3\left(\frac{6x-3}{3}\right) - 3(9x + 9)$

E. $15x - 9 \neq 3\left(\frac{6x-3}{3}\right) - 3(9x + 9)$

49. C: The side of the square is equal to the diameter of the circle, or twice the radius, that is, $2r$. The area of the square is this quantity squared, or $4r^2$. The area of the circle is, πr^2. Subtracting gives the difference between the two areas, $\Delta A = 4r^2 - \pi r^2 = r^2(4 - \pi)$.

A. $2\pi \neq r^2(4 - \pi)$

B. $\frac{4}{3}\pi r^3 \neq r^2(4 - \pi)$

D. $2\pi r \neq r^2(4 - \pi)$

E. $2r^2 \neq r^2(4 - \pi)$

50. E: There are 90 two-digit numbers (all integers from, and including, 10 to, and including, 99). Of those, there are 13 multiples of 7: 14, 21, 28, 35, 42, 49, 56, 63, 70, 77, 84, 91, 98.

Science

1. A: Diffusion is fastest through gases. The next fastest medium for diffusion is liquid, followed by plasma, and then solids. In chemistry, diffusion is defined as the movement of matter by the random motions of molecules. In a gas or a liquid, the molecules are in perpetual motion. For instance, in a quantity of seemingly immobile air, molecules of nitrogen and oxygen are constantly bouncing off each other. There is even some miniscule degree of diffusion in solids, which rises in proportion to the temperature of the substance.

2. B: The oxidation number of the hydrogen in CaH_2 is –1. The oxidation number is the positive or negative charge of a monoatomic ion. In other words, the oxidation number is the numerical charge on an ion. An ion is a charged version of an element. Oxidation number is often referred to as oxidation state. Oxidation number is sometimes used to describe the number of electrons that must be added or removed from an atom in order to convert the atom to its elemental form.

3. A: Boron does not exist as a diatomic molecule. The other possible answer choices, fluorine, oxygen, and nitrogen, all exist as diatomic molecules. A diatomic molecule always appears in nature as a pair: The word *diatomic* means "having two atoms." With the exception of astatine, all of the halogens are diatomic. Chemistry students often use the mnemonic BrINClHOF (pronounced "brinkelhoff") to remember all of the diatomic elements: bromine, iodine, nitrogen, chlorine, hydrogen, oxygen, and fluorine. Note that not all of these diatomic elements are halogens.

4. D: Hydriodic acid is another name for aqueous HI. In an aqueous solution, the solvent is water. Hydriodic acid is a polyatomic ion, meaning that it is composed of two or more elements. When this solution has an increased amount of oxygen, the *-ate* suffix on the first word is converted to *-ic*. This process can be quite complex, so you should carefully review this material before your exam.

5. A: A limiting reactant is entirely used up by the chemical reaction. Limiting reactants control the extent of the reaction and determine the quantity of the product. A reducing agent is a substance that reduces the amount of another substance by losing electrons. A reagent is any substance used in a chemical reaction. Some of the most common reagents in the laboratory are sodium hydroxide and hydrochloric acid. The behavior and properties of these substances are known, so they can be effectively used to produce predictable reactions in an experiment.

6. B: The horizontal rows of the periodic table are called periods. The vertical columns of the periodic table are known as groups or families. All of the elements in a group have similar properties. The relationships between the elements in each period are similar as you move from left to right. The periodic table was developed by Dmitri Mendeleev to organize the known elements according to their similarities. New elements can be added to the periodic table without necessitating a redesign.

7. C: The mass of 7.35 mol water is 132 grams. You should be able to find the mass of various chemical compounds when you are given the number of mols. The information required to perform this function is included on the periodic table. To solve this problem, find the molecular mass of water by finding the respective weights of hydrogen and oxygen. Remember that water contains two hydrogen molecules and one oxygen molecule. The molecular mass of hydrogen is roughly 1, and the molecular mass of oxygen is roughly 16. A molecule of water, then, has approximately 18 grams of mass. Multiply this by 7.35 mol, and you will obtain the answer 132.3, which is closest to answer choice C.

8. D: Of these orbitals, the last to fill is 6s. Orbitals fill in the following order: 1s, 2s, 2p, 3s, 3p, 4s, 3d, 4p, 5s, 4d, 5p, 6s, 4f, 5d, 6p, 7s, 5f, 6d, and 7p. The number is the orbital number, and the letter is the sublevel identification. Sublevel s has one orbital and can hold a maximum of two electrons. Sublevel p has three orbitals and can hold a maximum of six electrons. Sublevel d has five orbitals and can hold a maximum of 10 electrons. Sublevel f has seven orbitals and can hold a maximum of 14 electrons.

9. D: The mass of 1.0 mol oxygen gas is 32 grams. The molar mass of oxygen can be obtained from the periodic table. In most versions of the table, the molar mass of the element is directly beneath the full name of the element. There is a little trick to this question. Oxygen is a diatomic molecule, which means that it always appears in pairs. In order to determine the mass in grams of 1.0 mol of oxygen gas, then, you must double the molar mass. The listed mass is 16, so the correct answer to the problem is 32.

10. D: Gamma radiation has no charge. This form of electromagnetic radiation can travel a long distance and can penetrate the human body. Sunlight and radio waves are both examples of gamma radiation. Alpha radiation has a 2+ charge. It only travels short distances and cannot penetrate clothing or skin. Radium and uranium both emit alpha radiation. Beta radiation has a 1– charge. It can travel several feet through the air and is capable of penetrating the skin. This kind of radiation can be damaging to health over a long period of exposure. There is no such thing as delta radiation.

11. A: When forward and reverse chemical reactions are taking place at the same rate, a chemical reaction has achieved equilibrium. This means that the respective concentrations of reactants and products do not change over time. In theory, a chemical reaction will remain in equilibrium indefinitely. One of the common tasks in the chemistry lab is to find the equilibrium constant (or set of relative concentrations that result in equilibrium) for a given reaction. In thermal equilibrium, there is no net heat exchange between a body and its surroundings. In dynamic equilibrium, any motion in one direction is offset by an equal motion in the other direction.

12. B: 119°K is equivalent to –154 degrees Celsius. To convert degrees Kelvin to degrees Celsius, simply subtract 273. To convert degrees Celsius to degrees Kelvin, simply add 273. To convert degrees Kelvin into degrees Fahrenheit, multiply by 9/5 and subtract 460. To convert degrees Fahrenheit to degrees Kelvin, add 460 and then multiply by 5/9. To convert degrees Celsius to degrees Fahrenheit, multiply by 9/5 and then add 32. To convert degrees Fahrenheit to degrees Celsius, subtract 32 and then multiply by 5/9.

13. B: The *joule* is the SI unit of energy. Energy is the ability to do work or generate heat. In regard to electrical energy, a joule is the amount of electrical energy required to pass a current of one ampere through a resistance of one ohm for one second. In physical or mechanical terms, the joule is the amount of energy required for a force of one newton to act over a distance of one meter. The *ohm* is a unit of electrical resistance. The *henry* is a unit of inductance. The *newton* is a unit of force.

14. A: A *mass spectrometer* separates gaseous ions according to their mass-to-charge ratio. This machine is used to distinguish the various elements in a piece of matter. An *interferometer* measures the wavelength of light by comparing the interference phenomena of two waves: an experimental wave and a reference wave. A *magnetometer* measures the direction and magnitude of a magnetic field. Finally, a *capacitance meter* measures the capacitance of a capacitor. Some sophisticated capacitance meters may also measure inductance, leakage, and equivalent series resistance.

15. C: Of the given materials, aluminum has the smallest specific heat. The specific heat of a substance is the amount of heat required to raise the temperature of one gram of the substance by one degree Celsius. In some cases, specific heat is expressed as a ratio of the heat required to raise the temperature of one gram of a substance by one degree Celsius to the heat required to raise the temperature of one gram of water by one degree Celsius.

16. C: In a *redox* reaction, also known as an oxidation-reduction reaction, electrons are transferred from one atom to another. A redox reaction changes the oxidation numbers of the atoms. In a *combustion* reaction, one material combines with an oxidizer to form a product and generate heat. In a *synthesis* reaction, multiple chemicals are combined to create a more complex product. In a *double-displacement* reaction, two chemical compounds trade bonds or ions and create two different compounds.

17. A: Van der Waals forces are the weak forces of attraction between two molecules. The van der Waals force is considered to be any of the attractive or repulsive forces between electrons that are not related to electrostatic interaction or covalent bonds. Compared to other chemical bonds, the strength of van der Waals forces is small. However, these forces have a great effect on a substance's solubility and other characteristics.

18. D: The number of protons in an atom is the atomic number. Protons are the fundamental positive unit of an atom. They are located in the nucleus. In a neutral atom (an atom with neither positive nor negative charge), the number of protons in the nucleus is equal to the number of electrons orbiting the nucleus. When it needs to be expressed, atomic number is written as a subscript in front of the element's symbol, for example in $_{13}$Al. Atomic mass, meanwhile, is the average mass of the various isotopes of a given element. Atomic identity and atomic weight are not concepts in chemistry.

19. B: It is impossible for an *AaBb* organism to have the *aa* combination in the gametes. It is impossible for each letter to be used more than one time, so it would be impossible for the lowercase *a* to appear twice in the gametes. It would be possible, however, for *Aa* to appear in the gametes, since there is one uppercase *A* and one lowercase *a*. Gametes are the cells involved in sexual reproduction. They are germ cells.

20. B: Water stabilizes the temperature of living things. The ability of warm-blooded animals, including human beings, to maintain a constant internal temperature is known as *homeostasis*. Homeostasis depends on the presence of water in the body. Water tends to minimize changes in temperature because it takes a while to heat up or cool down. When the human body gets warm, the blood vessels dilate and blood moves away from the torso and toward the extremities. When the body gets cold, blood concentrates in the torso. This is the reason why hands and feet tend to get especially cold in cold weather.

21. C: The sugar and phosphate in DNA are connected by covalent bonds. A *covalent bond* is formed when atoms share electrons. It is very common for atoms to share pairs of electrons. An *ionic bond* is created when one or more electrons are transferred between atoms. *Ionic bonds*, also known as *electrovalent bonds*, are formed between ions with opposite charges. There is no such thing as an *overt bond* in chemistry.

22. A: The second part of an organism's scientific name is its species. The system of naming species is called binomial nomenclature. The first name is the *genus*, and the second name is the *species*. In binomial nomenclature, species is the most specific designation. This system enables the same name to be used all around the world, so that scientists can communicate with one another. Genus and species are just two of the categories in biological classification, otherwise known as taxonomy. The levels of classification, from most general to most specific, are kingdom, phylum, class, order, family, genus, and species. As you can see, binomial nomenclature only includes the two most specific categories.

23. B: Unlike other organic molecules, lipids are not water soluble. Lipids are typically composed of carbon and hydrogen. Three common types of lipid are fats, waxes, and oils. Indeed, lipids usually feel oily when you touch them. All living cells are primarily composed of lipids, carbohydrates, and proteins. Some examples of fats are lard, corn oil, and butter. Some examples of waxes are beeswax and carnauba wax. Some examples of steroids are cholesterol and ergosterol.

24. D: *Hemoglobin* is not a steroid. It is a protein that helps to move oxygen from the lungs to the various body tissues. Steroids can be either synthetic chemicals used to reduce swelling and inflammation or sex hormones produced by the body. *Cholesterol* is the most abundant steroid in the human body. It is necessary for the creation of bile, though it can be dangerous if the levels in the body become too high. *Estrogen* is a female steroid produced by the ovaries (in females), testes (in males), placenta, and adrenal cortex. It contributes to adolescent sexual development, menstruation, mood, lactation, and aging. *Testosterone* is the main hormone produced by the testes; it is responsible for the development of adult male sex characteristics.

25. C: *Melatonin* is produced by the pineal gland. One of the primary functions of melatonin is regulation of the circadian cycle, which is the rhythm of sleep and wakefulness. *Insulin* helps regulate the amount of glucose in the blood. Without insulin, the body is unable to convert blood sugar into energy. *Testosterone* is the main hormone produced by the testes; it is responsible for the development of adult male sex characteristics. *Epinephrine*, also known as adrenaline, performs a number of functions: It quickens and strengthens the heartbeat and dilates the bronchioles. Epinephrine is one of the hormones secreted when the body senses danger.

26. C: *Ribosomes* are the organelles that organize protein synthesis. A ribosome, composed of RNA and protein, is a tiny structure responsible for putting proteins together. The *mitochondrion* converts chemical energy into a form that is more useful for the functions of the cell. The *nucleus* is the central structure of the cell. It contains the DNA and administrates the functions of the cell. The *vacuole* is a cell organelle in which useful materials (for example, carbohydrates, salts, water, and proteins) are stored.

27. C: Prokaryotic cells do not contain a nucleus. A *prokaryote* is simply a single-celled organism without a nucleus. It is difficult to identify the structures of a prokaryotic cell, even with a microscope. These cells are usually shaped like a rod, a sphere, or a spiral. A *eukaryote* is an organism containing cells with nuclei. Bacterial cells are prokaryotes, but since there are other kinds of prokaryotes, *bacteria* cannot be the correct answer to this question. *Cancer* cells are malignant, atypical cells that reproduce to the detriment of the organism in which they are located.

28. A: *Phenotype* is the physical presentation of an organism's genes. In other words, the phenotype is the physical characteristics of the organism. Phenotype is often contrasted with *genotype*, the genetic makeup of an organism. The genotype of the organism is not visible in its presentation, although some of the characteristics encoded in the genes have to do with physical presentation. A *phylum* is a group of classes that are closely related. A *species* is a group of like organisms that are capable of breeding together and producing similar offspring.

29. A: Bacterial cells do not contain *mitochondria*. Bacteria are prokaryotes composed of single cells; their cell walls contain peptidoglycans. The functions normally performed in the mitochondria are performed in the cell membrane of the bacterial cell. *DNA* is the nucleic acid that contains the genetic information of the organism. It is in the shape of a double helix. DNA can reproduce itself and can synthesize RNA. A *vesicle* is a small cavity containing fluid. A *ribosome* is a tiny particle composed of RNA and protein, in which polypeptides are constructed.

30. B: *Hemoglobin* is a protein. Proteins contain carbon, nitrogen, oxygen, and hydrogen. These substances are required for the growth and repair of tissue and the formation of enzymes. Hemoglobin is found in red blood cells and contains iron. It is responsible for carrying oxygen from the lungs to the various body tissues. *Adenosine triphosphate* (ATP) is a compound used by living organisms to store and use energy. *Estrogen* is a steroid hormone that stimulates the development of female sex characteristics. *Cellulose* is a complex carbohydrate that composes the better part of the cell wall.

31. D: Deoxyribonucleic acid (*DNA*) is not involved in translation. *Translation* is the process by which messenger RNA (*mRNA*) messages are decoded into polypeptide chains. Transfer RNA (*tRNA*) is a molecule that moves amino acids into the ribosomes during the synthesis of protein.

Messenger RNA carries sets of instructions for the conversion of amino acids into proteins from the RNA to the other parts of the cell. *Ribosomes* are the tiny particles in the cell where proteins are put together. Ribosomes are composed of ribonucleic acid (RNA) and protein.

32. C: There are four different nucleotides in DNA. *Nucleotides* are monomers of nucleic acids, composed of five-carbon sugars, a phosphate group, and a nitrogenous base. Nucleotides make up both DNA and RNA. They are essential for the recording of an organism's genetic information, which guides the actions of the various cells of the body. Nucleotides are also a crucial component of adenosine triphosphate (ATP), one of the parts of DNA and a chemical that enables metabolism and muscle contractions.

33. B: *Red blood cells* do not have a nucleus. These cells are shaped a little like a doughnut, although the hole in the center is not quite open. The other three types of cell have a nucleus. *Platelets*, which are fragments of cells and are released by the bone marrow, contribute to blood clotting. *White blood cells*, otherwise known as leukocytes, help the body fight disease. A *phagocyte* is a cell that can entirely surround bacteria and other microorganisms. The two most common phagocytes are neutrophils and monocytes, both of which are white blood cells.

34. D: *Fission* is the process of a bacterial cell splitting into two new cells. Fission is a form of asexual reproduction in which an organism divides into two components; each of these two parts will develop into a distinct organism. The two cells, known as daughter cells, are identical. *Mitosis*, on the other hand, is the part of eukaryotic cell division in which the cell nucleus divides. In *meiosis*, the homologous chromosomes in a diploid cell separate, reducing the number of chromosomes in each cell by half. In *replication*, a cell creates duplicate copies of DNA.

35. D: The epiglottis covers the trachea during swallowing, thus preventing food from entering the airway. The trachea, also known as the windpipe, is a cylindrical portion of the respiratory tract that joins the larynx with the lungs. The esophagus connects the throat and the stomach. When a person swallows, the esophagus contracts to force the food down into the stomach. Like other structures in the respiratory system, the esophagus secretes mucus for lubrication.

36. B: The epidermis is the outermost layer of skin. The thickness of this layer of skin varies over different parts of the body. For instance, the epidermis on the eyelids is very thin, while the epidermis over the soles of the feet is much thicker. The dermis lies directly beneath the epidermis. It is composed of collagen, elastic tissue, and reticular fibers. Beneath the dermis lies the subcutaneous tissue, which consists of fat, blood vessels, and nerves. The subcutaneous tissue contributes to the regulation of body temperature. The hypodermis is the layer of cells underneath the dermis; it is generally considered to be a part of the subcutaneous tissue.

37. D: Of the given structures, veins have the lowest blood pressure. *Veins* carry oxygen-poor blood from the outlying parts of the body to the heart. An *artery* carries oxygen-rich blood from the heart to the peripheral parts of the body. An *arteriole* extends from an artery to a capillary. A *venule* is a tiny vein that extends from a capillary to a larger vein.

38. C: Of the four heart chambers, the left ventricle is the most muscular. When it contracts, it pushes blood out to the organs and extremities of the body. The right ventricle pushes blood into the lungs. The atria, on the other hand, receive blood from the outlying parts of the body and transport it into the ventricles. The basic process works as follows: Oxygen-poor blood fills the right atrium and is pumped into the right ventricle, from which it is pumped into the pulmonary artery and on to the lungs. In the lungs, this blood is oxygenated. The blood then reenters the heart at the left atrium, which when full pumps into the left ventricle. When the left ventricle is full, blood is pushed into the aorta and on to the organs and extremities of the body.

39. A: The *cerebrum* is the part of the brain that interprets sensory information. It is the largest part of the brain. The cerebrum is divided into two hemispheres, connected by a thin band of tissue called the corpus callosum. The *cerebellum* is positioned at the back of the head, between the brain stem and the cerebrum. It controls both voluntary and involuntary movements. The *medulla oblongata* forms the base of the brain. This part of the brain is responsible for blood flow and breathing, among other things.

40. A: An adult inhales 500 mL of air in an average breath. Interestingly, humans can inhale about eight times as much air in a single breath as they do in an average breath. People tend to take a larger breath after making a larger inhalation. This is one reason that many breathing therapies, for instance those incorporated into yoga practice, focus on making a complete exhalation. The process of respiration is managed by the autonomic nervous system. The body requires a constant replenishing of oxygen, so even brief interruptions in respiration can be damaging or fatal.

41. C: Forty percent of female blood volume is composed of red blood cells. Red blood cells, otherwise known as erythrocytes, are large and do not have a nucleus. These cells are produced in the bone marrow and carry oxygen throughout the body. White blood cells, also known as leukocytes, make up about 1% of the blood volume. About 55% of the blood volume is made up of plasma, which itself is primarily composed of water. The plasma in blood supplies cells with nutrients and removes metabolic waste. Blood also contains platelets, otherwise known as thrombocytes, which are essential to effective blood clotting.

42. D: The graph shows that temperatures in the lower stratosphere are -50°C or lower, permitting more efficient engine operation. The text indicates that 75% of the Earth's atmosphere is in the troposphere, which is below the stratosphere. It also states that convective mixing of air, and therefore the effects of weather, are characteristic of the troposphere. In the stratosphere, temperature-based layering of air leads to a stable environment. All of these effects combine to allow jets to operate with the best fuel efficiency possible in the lower reaches of the atmosphere.

43. D: This can be read from the graph. The thermosphere contains both the coldest and the highest temperatures in the atmospheric regions beneath outer space. In the thermosphere, atmospheric gases form layers of relatively pure molecular species. In its lower reaches, CO2 contributes to cooling through radiative emission, as in the mesosphere. In its upper reaches, molecular oxygen absorbs solar radiation and causes significant warming.

44. A: A solar eclipse is when the moon moves between the Sun and the Earth. When viewed from the Earth, the moon and the Sun are about the same size, and thus the moon can completely block the sun.

45. C: Pollination is the fertilization of plants. It involves the transfer of pollen from the anther to the stigma, either by wind or by insects.

46. B: Movement of the ground, or an earthquake, generates seismic waves. These movements can be detected with a sensitive instrument called a seismograph.

47. A: A food chain shows how energy is transferred from one organism to another. A producer uses the energy from the sun to make its own food. Most of the energy in a food chain is in the level of the producer.

48. D: The *electron transport system* enacted during aerobic respiration requires oxygen. This is the last component of biological oxidation. *Osmosis* is the movement of fluid from an area of high concentration through a partially permeable membrane to an area of lower concentration. This process usually stops when the concentration is the same on either side of the membrane. *Glycolysis* is the initial step in the release of glucose energy. The *Krebs cycle* is the last phase of the process in which cells convert food into energy. It is during this stage that carbon dioxide is produced and hydrogen is extracted from molecules of carbon.

49. A: The property of cohesion is responsible for the passage of water through a plant. *Cohesion* is the attractive force between two molecules of the same substance. The water in the roots of the plant is drawn upward into the stem, leaves, and flowers by the presence of other water molecules. *Adhesion* is the attractive force between molecules of different substances. *Osmosis* is a process in which water diffuses through a selectively permeable membrane. *Evaporation* is the conversion of water from a liquid to a gas.

50. B: Oxygen is not one of the products of the Krebs cycle. The *Krebs cycle* is the second stage of cellular respiration. In this stage, a sequence of reactions converts pyruvic acid into carbon dioxide. This stage of cellular respiration produces the phosphate compounds that provide most of the energy for the cell. The Krebs cycle is also known as the citric acid cycle or the tricarboxylic acid cycle.

Social Studies

HISTORY

1. D: The Platt Amendment of 1899 granted the United States the right to intervene in Cuban affairs and maintain a presence on the island. Hawaii was annexed shortly before the Spanish-American War. U.S. imperialism was accelerated following McKinley's assassination. The Boxer Rebellion of 1900 took place in China and preceded the Russo-Japanese War, which began in 1904.

2. A: Brown v. Board of Education was decided in 1954. Rosa Parks was arrested in 1955. The lunch counter sit-ins were staged in 1960. The March on Washington took place in 1963.

3. B: The term "Manifest Destiny" originated with the annexation of Texas as Americans began to envision a nation that spread from coast to coast. Texas entered the union as a slave state. The Monroe Doctrine addressed European intervention in the Western Hemisphere, which was not an issue in the annexation of Texas. Mexican resentment of the annexation was a factor in the Mexican War, which began the following year.

4. A: In 1985, Mikhail Gorbachev's programs of "glasnost," or openness, and "perestroika," or economic restructuring, led to an increase in free speech and free enterprise throughout the Soviet Union. By 1991, these reforms had led to the collapse of Communist power in Russia and the dissolution of the Soviet Union. Russia and the other newly independent states that comprised the former Soviet Union suffered great economic hardship following the breakup. With the collapse of the Soviet Union as a world power, the Cold War that began after World War II came to an end. The bloody conflict in Bosnia (1992-1995) was caused in part by the weakening of Communist control in Yugoslavia at the end of the Cold War.

5. D: In the Dred Scott decision of 1857, the Court ruled that no slave or descendent of slaves could ever be a United States citizen. It also declared the Missouri Compromise of 1820 to be unconstitutional, clearing the way for the expansion of slavery in new American territories. This ruling pleased Southerners and outraged the North further dividing the nation and setting the stage for war.

6. B: All of these acts of Parliament were intended to raise revenue at the expense of the colonies. The colonists challenged Parliament's right to levy tax on them without their express consent.

7. D: In his extremely influential pamphlet *Common Sense*, Paine argued persuasively against all forms of monarchy and aristocracy. He advocated the formation of a republic that derives its power exclusively from the governed. While the European writers also advocated government that derives its authority from the people, none went as far as Paine in proposing the total abolition of the traditional noble classes.

8. D: Without the power of taxation, the new federal government had to rely on the states to provide the money needed to wage war against England and to pay the huge national debt accrued during the Revolution. The power to raise revenues through taxation was an essential feature of the subsequent Constitution.

9. D: Indentured servants agreed to work for a set period of time in exchange for transportation to the New World and such basic necessities as food and shelter. They did not receive wages and were generally not highly-educated people. Employers often viewed indentured servants with scorn and treated them as harshly as they treated slaves.

10. D: Madison proposed nineteen amendments to the first Congress in 1789 twelve of which were sent to the states and ten officially ratified in 1791. Neither Adams nor Jefferson was present at the Constitutional Convention.

11. D: The Portuguese prince called Henry the Navigator launched the Age of Exploration with his voyage of 1419. He was followed by such notable Portuguese sailors as Bartholomeu Dias and Vasco de Gama, but Portuguese fortunes waned in the ensuing centuries as Spanish and Dutch exploration gained in prominence.

12. C: Sinclair's 1906 novel sparked public outrage by exposing the dehumanizing and unsanitary conditions prevalent in the American meatpacking industry at the turn of the century. Norris's 1901 novel depicted the conflict between wheat growers and corrupt railroad officials in California. Riis documented life in the slums of New York City in the 1880s. Steffens's muckraking journalism exposed political corruption across the country in the early years of the 20th century.

13. A: The First Amendment addresses freedom of speech, assembly, religion and the freedom of the press. A speedy trial is covered in the Sixth Amendment, cruel and unusual punishment in the Eighth Amendment, and search and seizure in the Fourth Amendment.

14. C: The FDIC and the SEC were both New Deal agencies created by the FDR administration in response to the stock market crash and bank failures of the Great Depression era. Both agencies still play an important role in maintaining public confidence in the nation's fundamental economic institutions.

15. C: The Quartering Act required colonists to provide food and shelter to British soldiers. Unlike the other mentioned acts, it did not impose a tax on sugar, coffee, tea, printed materials, or other items in common use by the colonists.

16. A: On March 5, 1770 angry colonists in Boston threw snowballs at a British officer. The violence quickly escalated, and the soldiers commanded by Captain Preston eventually fired on the crowd and killed several people. The silversmith and engraver Paul Revere engraved a depiction of the event and wrote an inflammatory poem to accompany his engraving. The Boston Tea Party took place over three years later. Revere's famous ride to announce the movement of the British army took place in 1775, and the Battle of Lexington and Concord, which was the first military engagement of the American Revolution, was fought the same day.

17. B: Charles Schenck was arrested for distributing leaflets advocating opposition to the draft during World War I. The Supreme Court unanimously decided that free speech could be restricted if it creates "a clear and present danger." This ruling was subsequently modified by Brandenburg v. Ohio in 1969. Plessy supported the "separate but equal" doctrine; Engle ruled that school prayer was unconstitutional; Miranda required police to advise criminal suspects of their rights.

18. A: Nationalistic conflicts arose in 1990 when Slovenia and Croatia declared independence from Yugoslavia. A civil war between Croatians and Serbians was followed by an outbreak of violence between Serbians and the Muslims of Bosnia-Herzegovina. In 1995, leaders of Bosnia, Croatia, and Serbia met for 21 days in Dayton, Ohio and agreed to the creation of separate Serb and Bosnian states. Unfortunately, relationships in the region remain unstable.

19. B: Plessy v. Ferguson (1896) found that segregated facilities for blacks and whites are not in violation of the Constitution. The doctrine of "separate but equal" was overturned in Brown v. Board of Education (1954). Marbury v. Madison (1803) established the Supreme Court's power to strike down acts of Congress that conflict with the Constitution. Gideon v. Wainwright (1963) guaranteed an attorney to anyone charged with a serious criminal offense.

20. B: King William's War, which was fought between 1689 and 1697, included quite a few violent border attacks by Indians in America, but no major army battles. The Treaty of Ryswick ending this war did not make any changes in territories. Queen Anne's War (a), which lasted from 1702 to 1713, was fought against France and Spain. It was ended by the Treaty of Utrecht, which ceded much territory to England. King George's War (c), which lasted from 1739 to 1748, involved major army battles on American soil. American soldiers went on a number of expeditions with British troops. The Treaty of Aix-la Chapelle ended this war. In it, England returned Louisbourg to France, trading it for territories on the Indian continent. The French and Indian War (d), which lasted from 1754 to 1763, featured many army battles on American soil. The 1763 Treaty of Paris ending this war ceded all of France's territories in Canada and North America to England.

Economics

1. B: Economists understand the true cost of an action as not only its monetary cost but the cost of other opportunities missed as a result of pursuing that action. For example, if a person chooses to go to school rather than working, the cost of the action involves not only tuition and other associated fees and expenses, but the money one would have earned working, as well as the time one could have spent pursuing other activities. The concept of opportunity cost is not described by options A, C, or D, each of which is concerned only with monetary costs. Each of these answers can be rejected on that basis.

2. B: Unemployment leads to lost productivity because people who would be productive if employed (thus contributing to economic growth) are not economically productive when they do not have work. Option A can be rejected because high unemployment is not typically thought to be a central cause of inflation; rather, high levels of unemployment might instead contribute to deflation (an overall decrease in prices). Option C can be rejected because unemployment would tend to have the effect of decreasing aggregate demand rather than increasing it, simply because fewer people would have money with which to make purchases. Option D can be rejected because unemployment is less likely to increase aggregate supply than to reduce it (fewer people working means fewer people producing goods and services).

3. C: The graph shows a shift in demand, with a corresponding increase in the price of SuperCell Batteries. The shift is illustrated by the two demand curves, with Demand 2 curve illustrating an increase in price. Because the price has increased, not decreased, this eliminates option A. The equilibrium point is the point at which the quantity demanded equals the quantity supplied. The graph shows two equilibrium points, the first where Demand 1 meets the supply curve, and the second where Demand 2 meets the supply curve. Because equilibrium has shifted, option B can eliminated. Regarding option D, a double coincidence of wants occurs when two people each have a good or service the other wants, giving rise to the possibility of trade (without money). The graph does not illustrate anything regarding a double coincidence of wants, so option D can be rejected on that basis.

4. B: A strict constructionist, Jefferson argued that that the Constitution did not make any provision for the creation of a federal bank. Jefferson was a leader of the Democratic-Republicans who opposed the establishment of a powerful central government. He believed that the Bank would give an unfair advantage to the more industrial northern states.

5. A: Along with stock market speculation, a major cause of the Great Depression was an increased supply of cars, radios, and other goods that was not matched by consumer demand. Industrial production far exceeded the population's purchasing power. Farmers were plagued by overproduction and falling prices while international trade suffered from rising tariffs.

6. B: Keynesian economics is based on the notion that governments can effectively stimulate economic growth through taxation, adjustment of interest rates, and the funding of public projects. His economic philosophy contrasts sharply with the free-market philosophies of Smith, Hayek, and Friedman.

7. C: Formulated in the early 19th century, Malthus's theory that population increase would ultimately outpace increases in the means of subsistence did not anticipate technological advances in food production and birth control; nevertheless, the theory was highly influential in the formulation of subsequent economic and social policies.

8. B: Shared, or concurrent, powers are those powers held by both the states and the federal government. These include taxation, borrowing money, establishing courts, and making and enforcing laws. Implied powers are those assumed by the federal government based on the "elastic clause" in Article I of the Constitution. Expressed, or enumerated, powers are those specifically granted to the federal government in Article I, Section 8 of the Constitution—e.g., the right to coin money, declare war, and regulate interstate and foreign commerce. Reserved powers are reserved exclusively to the states.

9. B: In order to prosper, a nation should not try to increase its imports. Mercantilism is an economic theory including the idea that prosperity comes from a positive balance of international trade. For any one nation to prosper, that nation should increase its exports (c) but decrease its imports. Exporting more to other countries while importing less from them will give a country a positive trade balance. This theory assumes that money and wealth are identical (a) assets of a nation. In addition, this theory also assumes that the volume of global trade is an unchangeable quantity. Mercantilism dictates that a nation's government should apply a policy of economic protectionism (d) by stimulating more exports and suppressing imports. Some ways to do accomplish this task have included granting subsidies for exports and imposing tariffs on imports.

Mercantilism can be regarded as essentially the opposite of the free trade policies that have been encouraged in more recent years.

10. C: The Federal Reserve System takes actions and issues statements to ensure that the United States grows economically, while keeping prices stable and allowing full employment.

CIVICS AND GOVERNMENT

1. C: Line 3 best lists the kinds of cases over which the U.S. federal court system has jurisdiction. The U.S. federal court system has jurisdiction over cases involving constitutional law, bankruptcy, and disputes between states (the federal court system also has jurisdiction over cases concerning U.S. treaties and laws, among other types of cases). State courts have jurisdiction over most contract cases, most criminal cases, and most personal injury cases; this eliminates Line 1, Line 2, and Line 4, each of which list one of those kinds of cases as under the jurisdiction of the U.S. federal court system.

2. C: The main subject matter of civic responsibility is a person's responsibilities as a citizen. By contrast, the main subject matter of personal responsibility is one's responsibilities as a person. For example, keeping a promise to a friend is often a matter of personal responsibility because such a duty arises from the friendship. Serving on a jury when called to do so is an example of civic responsibility because such a duty arises from the person's citizenship. None of the other options given accurately describe the main subject matter of civic responsibility. For example, while a journalist might see accurate reporting of government actions as his or her civic responsibility, such reporting is not the main subject matter of civic responsibility, and is also a responsibility that arises from that journalist's employment. Similar reasoning applies to a person's responsibilities as a government worker. This eliminates options A and D. Civic responsibility does not primarily concern inter-government relations; this eliminates option B.

3. B: Under the Fifth Amendment to the U.S. Constitution, the government may not strip certain basic rights from citizens without following the law. In the language of the Fifth Amendment itself, a person shall not "be deprived of life, liberty, or property without due process of law." Of all the options, option C is the only one that accurately describes the concept of due process as understood in the Fifth Amendment. Because due process does not explicitly guarantee a trial by jury within a reasonable timeframe, nor equal protection under the law (concepts covered elsewhere in the Constitution), options A and C and be rejected. Option D can be rejected because the Constitution restricts the government's ability to take away certain rights without following the law, not without a "dire cause" (such as the threat of imminent attack).

4. B: The Electoral College officially elects the President and the Vice President. The number of electors, or Electoral College members, allotted to a state is equal to that state's total number of U.S. Senators and U.S. Representatives. A state with two U.S. Senators and one U.S. Representative, for example, would have three electors in the Electoral College. Because every state has two U.S. Senators and at least one U.S. Representative, every state has at least 3 electors in the Electoral College. Option B is the only option that correctly describes how a state's number of Electoral College voters is determined; neither the number of counties in a state, nor the number of State Secretaries is relevant to this number.

5. D: In a parliamentary form of government, the executive branch is essentially a committee of the legislative branch. This is the only answer that correctly describes the relation between the executive branch and another branch of the government. The executive branch is neither a committee of the judicial branch, nor is it appointed by the judicial branch; this eliminates options B and C. The executive branch does not appoint members of the legislative branch; this eliminates option A. In the parliamentary government in Great Britain, for example, the legislature elects the Prime Minister, and the members of the Prime Minister's Cabinet are also selected from members of the legislative branch (either the House of Commons or the House of Lords).

6. D: The Federal Reserve has the power to buy and sell government bonds to or from banks, thereby raising or reducing interest rates. When banks buy government bonds, they have less money available to loan, and interest rates are higher; when banks sell bonds, they have more money available to loan, and interest rates are lower. Option A does accurately describe a tool of the Federal Reserve, but not a tool the Federal Reserve uses frequently; the same is true of option C, and therefore both options A and C can be rejected. Option D can be eliminated because the Federal Reserve does not buy or sell stock options to change interest rates.

7. A: Corporations offer limited liability protection, unlike sole proprietorships. For example, the person running a corporation is not personally liable for the debts of a corporation to the extent that a person running a sole proprietorship is for the debts of the proprietorship. In a sole proprietorship, the sole proprietor has unlimited liability for the debts of the business. Note that such debts include ordinary operating expenses, tax liability, liability from lawsuits, etc. Option B can be eliminated because corporations run afoul of the "double tax" problem, when the person running a corporation (who pays himself from the company earnings) pays tax on the company's earnings twice, first via the taxes assessed against corporation itself and second via his or her own personal income tax. Corporations are more expensive to form than sole proprietorships, but this is a disadvantage; this eliminates option C. Option D can be eliminated because corporations are more difficult to dissolve than sole proprietorships.

8. C: Mercantilism is the economic theory that nations advance the goal of accumulating capital by maintaining a balance of trade such that the value of exports exceeds that of imports. Great Britain maintained colonies to provide an inexpensive source of raw materials while creating markets for the goods manufactured in England. Under free trade, governments refrain from hindering the international exchange of goods and services. Nations that are granted most favored nation status are assured of enjoying equal advantages in international trade. A laissez-faire capitalist economy would theoretically be completely free of government regulation.

9. A: Article II of the Constitution gives the House of Representatives the sole power of impeachment and the Senate the sole power to convict. The Chief Justice of the United States is empowered to preside over the Senate trial of a President.

10. A: Checks and balances prevent any branch of the government from running roughshod over the other two. Separation of powers refers to the distribution of specific powers among the three branches of government. Judicial review is the power of the courts to overturn legislative or executive acts that are deemed unconstitutional. Advice and consent is the power to advise the President, ratify treaties, and confirm nominations, which is granted to the Senate in Article II of the Constitution.

11. D: The process of overriding a Presidential veto is described in Article I, Section 7, of the Constitution.

12. B: Shared, or concurrent, powers are those powers held by both the states and the federal government. While the Constitution specifically grants Congress the exclusive power to coin money, it does not specifically forbid the states from building roads, collecting taxes, and establishing courts.

Geography

1. A: Maine was the northern part of the Massachusetts Bay colony and subsequently part of the Commonwealth of Massachusetts. It became a state in 1820 as a result of the Missouri Compromise.

2. D: The taiga, or boreal forest, is found only in the North Temperate Zone between the tundra and the steppes. The largest biome on land, it is characterized by coniferous forests and stretches across the northern regions of North America and Eurasia. Deserts, savannas, and tropical rainforests are all found at lower latitudes within the Torrid Zone.

3. C: Mexico is the second largest producer of oil in the Western Hemisphere while Venezuela has the largest oil reserves in South America. Bolivia, Guatemala, and Uruguay are not petroleum-producing nations.

4. B: A topographic map uses contour lines to show the shape and elevation of the land. Political maps identify state and national boundaries as well as capitals and major cities. Resource maps show the natural resources and economic activities in a region. Road maps are used mainly for driving directions and trip planning.

5. C: Lying at a little more than 23° south of the equator, the Tropic of Capricorn is the border between the Southern Temperate Zone to the south and the Tropical Zone to the north. The southern hemisphere is tilted toward the sun to its maximum extent each year at the winter solstice in December. The northernmost latitude at which the sun can appear directly overhead is at the Tropic of Cancer during the summer solstice. The northern and southern hemispheres are separated by the equator at 0° degrees latitude. The eastern and western hemispheres are separated by the prime meridian at 0° longitude.

6. D: The Erie Canal was officially opened on October 26, 1825, and connected the Hudson River to Lake Erie. The Cayuga-Seneca Canal (a) connecting the Erie Canal to Cayuga Lake and Seneca Lake was first used in 1828. The Chambly Canal (b) is a Canadian canal in Quebec that was opened in 1843. It is not a part of the New York State Canal System, as the other canals listed here are. The Oswego Canal (c), which connects the Erie Canal to Lake Ontario at Oswego, was opened in 1828. The Barge Canal replaced the original Erie Canal in 1918 with a larger waterway. In 1992, the New York State Barge Canal was renamed the New York State Canal System, which incorporates all of the canals listed in this question except for the Chambly Canal (b), which is not in New York State.

7. D: The Mojave Desert is located in the United States.

8. C: About 30 percent of the surface of the Earth is covered by land.

Thank You

We at Mometrix would like to extend our heartfelt thanks to you, our friend and patron, for allowing us to play a part in your journey. It is a privilege to serve people from all walks of life who are unified in their commitment to building the best future they can for themselves.

The preparation you devote to these important testing milestones may be the most valuable educational opportunity you have for making a real difference in your life. We encourage you to put your heart into it—that feeling of succeeding, overcoming, and yes, conquering will be well worth the hours you've invested.

We want to hear your story, your struggles and your successes, and if you see any opportunities for us to improve our materials so we can help others even more effectively in the future, please share that with us as well. **The team at Mometrix would be absolutely thrilled to hear from you!** So please, send us an email (support@mometrix.com) and let's stay in touch.

If you feel as though you need additional help, please check out the other resources we offer:

Study Guide: http://MometrixStudyGuides.com/HiSET

Flashcards: http://MometrixFlashcards.com/HiSET

Made in the USA
Monee, IL
04 June 2020